Norwegian
phrase book & dictionary

439.8283421 Nor

Norwegian phrase book &
dictionary.

PRICE: $10.16 (3559/he)

Berlit
New York L

No part of this book may be reproduced, stored in a retrieval system or transmitted in any form or means electronic, mechanical, photocopying, recording or otherwise, without prior written permission from APA Publications.

Contacting the Editors
Every effort has been made to provide accurate information in this publication, but changes are inevitable. The publisher cannot be responsible for any resulting loss, inconvenience or injury. We would appreciate it if readers would call our attention to any errors or outdated information. We also welcome your suggestions; if you come across a relevant expression not in our phrase book, please contact us at: **comments@berlitzpublishing.com**

All Rights Reserved
© 2007 Berlitz Publishing/APA Publications (UK) Ltd.
Berlitz Trademark Reg. U.S. Patent Office and other countries. Marca Registrada. Used under license from Berlitz Investment Corporation.

Eleventh Printing: June 2012
Printed in China

Publishing Director: Mina Patria
Commissioning Editor: Kate Drynan
Editorial Assistant: Sophie Cooper
Translation: updated by Wordbank
Cover Design: Beverley Speight
Interior Design: Beverley Speight
Production Manager: Raj Trivedi
Picture Researcher: Lucy Johnston
Cover Photo: All photos Glyn Genin/APA, except iStock currency shot

Interior Photos: All photos Glyn Genin/APA, except iStock 17, 37, 47, 48, 121, 141, 146, 148, 151,152, 155, 159, 160, 163, 164, 173; Mina Patria 24; Greg Gladman 123; Beverley Speight 145; James Macdonald/APA 177

Contents

Food & Drink

People

Leisure Time

Special Requirements

In an Emergency

Dictionary

Pronunciation

This section is designed to make you familiar with the sounds of Norwegian by using our simplified phonetic transcription. You'll find the pronunciation of the Norwegian letters explained below, together with their 'imitated' equivalents (the Norwegian alphabet is the same as in English, with the addition of the letters æ, ø and å). This phonetic system is used throughout the phrase book; simply read the pronunciation as if it were English, noting any special rules below.

Stress has been indicated in the phonetic transcription with underlining, tone with the accent marks and long vowels with bold.

Consonants

Letter	Approximate Pronunciation	Symbol	Example	Pronunciation
g	1. before i and y, (sometimes before ei) like y in yes	y	gi	*yee*
	2. elsewhere, like g in go	g	gått	*goht*
gj	like y in yes	y	gjest	*yehst*
j	like y in yes	y	ja	*yah*
k	1. before i, y and ei like h in hue, but with the tongue raised a little higher	kh	kino	*khee´•nu*
	2. elsewhere, like k in kit	k	kaffe	*kahf´•fuh*
kj	like h in hue, but with the tongue raised a little higher	kh	kjøre	*khur`•ruh*

Letter	Approximate Pronunciation	Symbol	Example	Pronunciation
r	rolled near the front of the mouth	r	**rare**	_rah_` •ruh_
s	like s in sit	s	**spise**	_spee_` •suh_
sj	like sh in shut	sh	**stasjon**	stah•_shoo_´n
sk	1. before i and y (sometimes before øy), like sh in shut	sh	**ski**	shee
	2. elsewhere, like sk in skate	sk	**skole**	_skoo_` •luh_
skj	like sh in shut	sh	**skje**	sheh
w	like v in vice	v	**whisky**	_vihs_´ •kih_
z	like s in sit	s	**zoom**	soom

Letters b, c, d, f, h, l, m, n, p, q, t, v, x are generally pronounced as in English.

Vowels

Letter	Approximate Pronunciation	Symbol	Example	Pronunciation
a	1. like a in father, but longer	ah	**tak**	tahk
	2. like a in father	ah	**takk**	tahk
e	1. like e in get, but longer	eh	**sent**	sehnt
	2. like e in get	eh	**penn**	pehn
	3. like a in bad	a	**her**	har
	4. before r, like a in bad	a	**herre**	_ha_` •ruh_
	5. like u in uncle	uh	**sitte**	_sih_` •tuh_

Letter	Approximate Pronunciation	Symbol	Example	Pronunciation
i	1. like ee in bee	ee	**hit**	*heet*
	2. like i in sit	ih	**sitt**	*siht*
o	1. like oo in soon, with lips tightly rounded	oo	**ord**	*oor*
	2. like aw in saw	aw	**tog**	*tawg*
	3. like u i put, with lips tightly rounded	u	**ost**	*ust*
	4. like o in cloth	oh	**stoppe**	*stohp`•puh*
	5. before r, like oo in soon	oo	**hvor**	*voor*
u	1. like ew in few, but longer	ew	**mur**	*mewr*
	2. like ew in few	ew	**busk**	*bewsk*
	3. like u in put, with lips tightly rounded	u	**bukk**	*buk*
y	1. like ui in fruit, but longer	ui	**myr**	*muir*
	2. like ui in fruit	ui	**bygge**	*buig`•guh*
æ	1. like a in bad, but longer	a	**lære**	*la`•ruh*
	2. like a in bad	a	**færre**	*far´•ruh*
ø	1. like ur in fur, but longer and with lips rounded	ur	**blø**	*blur*
	2. like ur in fur, with lips rounded	ur	**sønn**	*surn*

Letter	Approximate Pronunciation	Symbol	Example	Pronunciation
å	1. like aw in saw, but longer	aw	såpe	_saw_`•puh_
	2. like o in cloth	oh	gått	goht

Vowel Combinations

Letter	Approximate Pronunciation	Symbol	Example	Pronunciation
ai	like ie in tie	ie	mais	mies
au	like ev in ever	ev	sau	sev
ei	like ay in say	ay	geit	yayt
eg	at the end of a word and before n, like ay in say	ay	jeg	yay
oi	like oi in oil	oi	koie	_koi_`•uh_
øy	like ur + y	ury	høy	hury

In Norwegian, vowel length distinguishes meaning. All vowels come in two lengths, long and short. Long vowels are in bold throughout the phonetics.

Norwegian is a tonal language. This means that tone is used to distinguish between certain words, which otherwise would sound the same. For example:

hender (_hehn´•nuhr_), tone 1 = plural of **hånd** (hand)
hender (_hehn`•nuhr_), tone 2 = present tense of **hende** (happen)

In the phonetics, tone 1, which is a rising tone (i.e., starts low and rises in pitch) is marked with the acute accent (´); tone 2, which is a falling tone (i.e., starts high and lowers in pitch), with the grave accent (`).

In Norwegian, consonants are silent in the following situations:
1. The letter **d** is generally silent after **l**, **n** or **r** (e.g. **holde**, **land**, **gård**), and sometimes at the end of words (e.g. **god**, **med**).
2. The letter **g** is silent in the endings **-lig** and **-ig**.
3. The letter **h** is silent when followed by a consonant (e.g. **hjem**, **hva**).
4. The letter **t** is silent in the definite form ('the') of neuter nouns (e.g., **eplet**) and in the pronoun **det**.
5. The letter **v** is silent in certain words (e.g. **selv**, **tolv**, **halv**).
6. In the eastern part of Norway the letter **r** is silent when followed by **l**, **n**, **s**, **t** (and sometimes **d**). These consonants are pronounced with the tip of the tongue turned up well behind the front teeth. The **r** then ceases to be pronounced, but influences the tone of the following consonant. This 'retroflex' pronunciation also occurs in words ending with an **r** if the following word begins with a **d**, **l**, **n**, **s** or **t**.

How to use this Book

> Sometimes you see two alternatives separated by a slash. Choose the one that's right for your situation.

ESSENTIAL

I'm here on vacation [holiday]/business. | **Jeg er her på ferie/i forretninger.** *yay ar ha, paw feh´r•yuh/ih fohr•reht´•nihng•uhr*
I'm going to... | **Jeg reiser til...** *yay rays`•uhr tihl...*
I'm staying at the...Hotel. | **Jeg bor på Hotell...** *yay boor paw hu•tehl´..*

> Words you may see are shown in YOU MAY SEE boxes.

YOU MAY SEE...

BUSSHOLDEPLASS/ | bus stop/tram stop
TRIKKEHOLDEPLASS |
INNGANG/UTGANG | enter/exit
STEMPLE BILLETTEN | stamp your ticket

> Any of the words or phrases listed can be plugged into the sentence below.

Tickets

Where's...? | **Hvor er det...?** *voor ar deh...*
the ATM | **en minibank** *ehn mee´•nih•bangk*
the bank | **en bank** *ehn bahngk*
the currency exchange office | **et vekslingskontor** *eht vehk`s•lihngs•kun•toor*

Norwegian phrases appear in purple.

Read the simplified pronunciation as if it were English. For more on pronunciation, see page 7.

Personal

Are you married?	**Er du gift?** *ar dew yihft*
I'm...	**Jeg er...** *yay ar...*
single	**singel** *ew`•yift*
in a relationship	**opptatt** *ohp´•taht*
married	**gift** *yift*
I'm widowed.	**Jeg er enkemann m /enke f.** *yay ar ehng`•kuh•mahn/ehng`•kuh*

For Numbers, see page 170.

Related phrases can be found by going to the page number indicated.

When different gender forms apply, the masculine form is followed by *m*; feminine by *f*

Norwegians tend to get right to business and don't engage in much small talk or socializing. You'll find them to be serious and direct in business dealings and in their manner of speaking in general.

Information boxes contain relevant country, culture and language tips.

Expressions you may hear are shown in You May Hear boxes.

YOU MAY HEAR...

Neste! *nehs`•tuh*	Next!
Billetten/Passet, takk. *bil•leht´•tuhn/pahs´•suh tahk*	Your ticket/passport, please.

Color-coded side bars identify each section of the book.

Survival

ESSENTIAL

I'm here on vacation [holiday]/business.	**Jeg er her på ferie/i forretninger.** *yay ar har paw feh´r•yuh/ih fohr•reht´•nihng•uhr*
I'm going to…	**Jeg reiser til…** *yay rays´•uhr tihl…*
I'm staying at the… Hotel.	**Jeg bor på Hotell…** *yay boor paw hu•tehl´…*

YOU MAY HEAR…

Billetten/Passet, takk. *bihl•leht´•tuhn/ pahs´•suh tahk*	Your ticket/passport, please.
Hva er formålet med reisen? *vah ar fohr`•maw•luh meh ray`•suhn*	What's the purpose of your trip?
Hvor skal du bo? *voor skahl dew boo*	Where are you staying?
Hvor lenge blir du? *voor lehng`•uh bleer dew*	How long are you staying?
Hvem reiser du sammen med? *vehm ray`•suhr dew sahm´•muhn meh*	Who are you with?

Border Control

I'm just passing through.	**Jeg er bare på gjennomreise.** *yay ar bah`•ruh paw yehn`•nohm•ray•suh*
I would like to declare…	**Jeg vil gjerne fortolle…** *yay vihl ya`r•nuh fohr•tohl´•luh…*
I have nothing to declare.	**Jeg har ingenting å fortolle.** *yay hahr ihng`•uhn• tihng aw fohr•tohl´•luh*

YOU MAY HEAR...

Har du noe å fortolle? _hahr dew noo`·uh aw fohr·tohl´·luh_ — Do you have anything to declare?

Du må betale toll for dette. _dew maw buh·tah´·luh tohl fohr deht`·tuh_ — You must pay duty on this.

Vær så snill å åpne denne bagen. _var saw snihl aw **aw**`p·nuh dehn`·nuh behg´·guhn_ — Please open this bag.

Money

ESSENTIAL

Where's...?	**Hvor er det...?** _voor **a**r deh..._
the ATM	**en minibank** _ehn **mee**´·nih·bangk_
the bank	**en bank** _ehn bahngk_
the currency exchange office	**et vekslingskontor** _eht vehk`s·lihngs·kun·**too**r_
What time does the bank open/close?	**Når åpner/stenger banken?** _nohr **aw**`p·nuhr/ stehng`·uhr bahng´·kuhn_
I'd like to change some dollars/pounds.	**Jeg vil gjerne veksle noen dollar/pund.** _yay vihl ya`r·nuh vehk`s·luh **noo**`·uhn dohl´·lahr/pewn_
I'd like to cash a traveler's check [cheque].	**Jeg vil gjerne løse inn en reisesjekk.** _yay vihl ya`r· nuh lur`·suh ihn ehn ray`·suh·shehk_

At the Bank

Can I exchange foreign currency here?	**Kan jeg veksle utenlandsk valuta her?** _kahn yay vehk`s·luh **ew**`·tuhn·lahnsk vah·lew´·tah har_

YOU MAY SEE...

The Norwegian currency is the **krone** (crown), abbreviated to **kr** or **NOK**, divided into 100 **øre**.
Coins: 50 **øre; kr** 1, 5, 10 and 20
Notes: **kr** 50, 100, 200, 500 and 1,000

What's the exchange rate?	**Hva er vekslingskursen?** *vah ar vehk`s•lihngs•kewr•suhn*
How much is the fee?	**Hvor mye tar dere i kommisjon?** *voor <u>mui</u>`•uh tahr deh`•ruh ih ku•mih•<u>shoo</u>´n*
I've lost my traveler's checks [cheques].	**Jeg har mistet reisesjekkene.** *yay hahr <u>mihs</u>`•tuht <u>ray</u>`•suh•shehk•kuh•nuh*
My card was lost.	**Jeg har mistet kortet.** *yay hahr <u>mihs</u>`•tuht <u>kohr</u>´•tuh*
My credit cards have been stolen.	**Kredittkortene mine ble stjålet.** *kreh•<u>diht</u>´•kohr•tuh•nuh <u>mee</u>`•nuh bleh <u>styaw</u>`•luht*
My card doesn't work.	**Kortet virker ikke.** *<u>kohr</u>´•tuh <u>vihr</u>`•kuhr <u>ihk</u>`•kuh*
The ATM ate my card.	**Minibanken spiste kortet mitt.** *mee•nih•bangk•en spih•ste kurt•e miht*

Cash can be obtained from **minibank** (ATMs), which can be readily found in urban areas . Most major credit cards and some debit cards are accepted. You will need a PIN that is compatible with European machines, usually a four-digit, numeric code. ATMs offer good rates, though there may be hidden fees.

Vekslingskontor (currency exchange offices), banks and post offices are options for exchanging currency. Exchange offices are found at airports, train stations, ship terminals and in many tourist centers. Banks are generally open Monday to Friday 8:15 a.m. to 3:30 p.m., though some close later one day a week and hours may vary in the provinces. Remember to bring your passport, in case you are asked for identification.

ESSENTIAL

How do I get to town?	**Hvordan kommer jeg til byen?** _voor_´-dahn	
	kohm´-muhr yay tihl **bui**´-uhn	
Where is…?	**Hvor er…?** voor ar…	
the airport	**flyplassen** _flui_´-plahs-suhn	
the train station	**jernbanestasjonen** _ya`rn_-bah-nuh-stah-shoon-uhn	
the bus station	**busstasjonen** bews´-stah-shoon-uhn	
the subway [underground] station	**T-banestasjonen** _teh_´-bah-nuh-stah-shoon-uhn	
How far is it?	**Hvor langt er det?** voor _lahngt_ _ar_ deh	
Where can I buy tickets?	**Hvor kan jeg kjøpe billetter?** voor kahn yay	
	khur`-puh bihl-_leht_´-tuhr	
A one-way [single]/ round-trip [return] ticket.	**En enveisbillett/tur-returbillett.** ehn	
	ehn´-vays-bihl-leht/tewr-reh-_tew´r_-bil-leht	
How much?	**Hvor mye koster det?** voor _mui_`-uh kohs´-tuhr deh	
Are there any discounts?	**Er det noen rabatter?** _ar_ deh _noo_`-uhn rah-_baht_´-tuhr	
Which…?	**Hvilken…?** _vihl_´-kuhn…	
gate	**utgang** _ew´t_-gahng	
line	**linje** _lihn_`-yuh	
platform	**perrong** pehr-_rohng_´	
Where can I get a taxi?	**Hvor kan jeg få tak i en drosje?** voor kahn yay f**aw**	
	t**aw**k ih ehn _drohsh_`-uh	
Can you take me to this address?	**Kan du kjøre meg til denne adressen?** kahn d**ew**	
	khur`-ruh may tihl _dehn_`-nuh ahd-_rehs_´-suhn	
Where can I rent a car?	**Hvor kan jeg leie bil?** voor kahn yay _lay_`-uh b**ee**l	
Can I have a map?	**Kan jeg få et kart?** kahn yay f**aw** eht kahrt	

Tickets

When's…to Stavanger?	**Når går…til Stavanger?** *nohr gawr…tihl stah-vahng´-uhr*
the (first) bus	**(første) buss** *(furrs`-tuh) bews*
the (next) flight	**(neste) fly** *(nehs`-tuh) flui*
the (last) train	**(siste) tog** *(sihs`-tuh) tawg*
Where can I buy tickets?	**Hvor kan jeg kjøpe billetter?** *voor kahn yay khur`-puh bihl-leht´-tuhr*
One ticket/ please.	**En billett/To billetter, takk.** *ehn bihl-leht´/too bihl-leht´-tuhr tak*
For today/tomorrow.	**For i dag/i morgen.** *fohr ih-dahg/ih-mawr`-uhn*
A one-way [single]/ round-trip [return] ticket.	**En enveisbillett/tur-returbillett.** *ehn ehn´-vays-bihl-leht/tewr-reh-tew´r-bil-leht*
A first class/economy class ticket.	**En billett på første klasse/ turistklasse.** *ehn bihl-eht´ poh furrs`-tuh klahs`-suh/tew-rihst´-klahs-su*
How much?	**Hvor mye koster det?** *voor mui`-uh kohs`-tuhr deh*
Is there a discount for…?	**Er det noen rabatt for…?** *ar deh noo`-uhn rah-baht´ fohr…*
children	**barn** *bahrn*
students	**studenter** *stew-dehn´-tuhr*
senior citizens	**pensjonister** *pahng-shoo-nihs´-tuhr*
The express bus/ express train, please.	**Ekspressbuss/ekspresstog, er du snill** *eks-pruhs-bews/eks-pruhs-tawg, ar dew snihl*
The local bus/train, please.	**Lokalbuss/-tog, er du snill** *loh-kahl-bews/tawg, ar dew snihl*
I have an e-ticket.	**Jeg har en e-billett.** *yay hahr ehn eh´-bihl-leht*
Can I buy a ticket on the bus/train?	**Kan man kjøpe billett på bussen/toget?** *kahn mahn khur`-puh bihl-leht´ poh bews´-suhn/taw´-guh*
Do I have to stamp the ticket before boarding?	**Må jeg stemple billetten før jeg går ombord?** *maw yay stam-pleh bill-eht-ehn fur yay gawr awm-bot*

YOU MAY HEAR...

Hvilket selskap flyr du med? *vihl`·kuht sehl`·skahp fluir dew meh* — What airline are you flying?

Innenlands eller utenlands? *ihn`·nuhn·lahns ehl`·luhr ew`·tuhn·lahns* — Domestic or international?

Hvilken terminal? *vihl`·kuhn tehr·mih·nahl`* — What terminal?

How long is this ticket valid?	**Hvor lenge er denne billetten gyldig?**	*voor lehn·geh ar dehn·neh beel·eht·ehn yil·deeg*
Can I return on the same ticket?	**Er det tur/retur?**	*ar deh tewr/reh·tewr*
I'd like to...my reservation.	**Jeg vil gjerne...reservasjonen.**	*yay vihl ya`r·nuh...reh·sehr·vah·shoo`n·uhn*
cancel	**annullere**	*ahn·newl·leh`·ruh*
change	**endre**	*ehn`·druh*
confirm	**bekrefte**	*buh·krehf`·tuh*

For Days, see page 172.
For Time, see page 171.

Plane

Airport Transfer

How much is a taxi to the airport?	**Hva koster drosje til flyplassen?**	*vah kohs`·tuhr drohsh`·uh tihl flui`·plahs·suhn*
To...Airport, please.	**Til...lufthavn.**	*tihl...lewft`·hahvn*
My airline is...	**Jeg flyr med...**	*yay fluir meh...*
My flight leaves at...	**Flyet mitt går...**	*flui`·uh miht gawr...*
I'm in a hurry.	**Jeg har dårlig tid.**	*yay hahr dawr`·lih teed*

Can you take an alternate route?	**Kan du kjøre en annen vei?** *kahn dew khur`•ruh eh• ahn`•nuhn vay*
Can you drive faster/ slower?	**Kan du kjøre fortere/saktere?** *kahn dew khur`•ruh foor`•tuh•ruh/sahk`•tuh•ruhw*

YOU MAY SEE…

ANKOMST	arrivals
AVGANG	departures
BAGASJEBÅND	baggage claim
SIKKERHETSVAKT	security
INNENLAND	domestic flights
UTLAND	international flights
INNSJEKKING	check-in
INNSJEKKING MED E-BILLETT	e-ticket check-in
GATE FOR AVGANG	departure gates

YOU MAY HEAR...

Neste! _nehs`·tuh_ — Next!

Billetten/Passet, takk. _bil·leht´·tuhn/ pahs´·suh tahk_ — Your ticket/passport, please.

Hvor mange kolli har du? _voor mang`·uh kohl´·lih hahr dew_ — How many pieces of luggage do you have?

Du har for mye bagasje. _dew hahr fohr mui´·uh bah·gah´·shuh_ — You have excess luggage.

Den er for tung/stor til håndbagasje. _dehn ar fohr tung/stoor tihl hohn`·bah·gah·shuh_ — That's too heavy/large for a carry-on [to carry on board].

Har du pakket disse veskene/ koffertene selv? _hahr dew pahk`·kuht dihs´·suh vehs`·kuh·nuh/kuf´·fuhr·tuh·nuh sehl_ — Did you pack these bags/ suitcases yourself?

Tar du med noe for andre? _tahr dew meh noo`·uh fohr ahn`·druh_ — Did anyone give you anything to carry?

Tøm lommene. _turm lum`·muh·nuh_ — Empty your pockets.

Ta av deg skoene. _tah ah day skoo´·uh·nuh_ — Take off your shoes.

Avgang…er nå klar for ombordstigning. _ahv`·gahng…ar naw klahr fohr ohm·boor´·steeg·nihng_ — Now boarding flight…

Checking In

Where's check-in? — **Hvor er innsjekkingsskranken?** _voor ar ihn´·shehk·kihngs·skrahng·kuhn_

My name is… — **Jeg heter…** _yay heh`·tuhr…_

I'm going to… — **Jeg skal til…** _yay skahl tihl…_

I have… — **Jeg har…** _yay hahr_

one suitcase — **en koffert** _ehn kohf·uhrt_

two suitcases	**to kofferter**	*toh kohf•uhrt•uhr*
one piece of hand luggage	**en håndbagasje**	*ehn hawn•bahg•ahsh•uh*
How much luggage is allowed?	**Hvor mye bagasje har man lov å ha med?**	*voor mui´•uh bah•gah´•shuh hahr mahn lawv oh hah me*
Is that pounds or kilos?	**Er det i pund eller kilo?**	*ar deht•uh ee pewn ehl•uhr shee•loh*
Which terminal?	**Hvilken terminal?**	*vee'k•uhn tar•mihn•ahl*
Which gate?	**Hvilken gate?**	*vee'k•uhn gayt*
Can I have a window/ an aisle seat?	**Kan jeg få plass ved vinduet/midtgangen?**	*kahn yay faw plahs veh vihn`•dew•uh/miht`•gahng•uhn*
When do we leave/ arrive?	**Når drar vi/kommer vi fram?**	*nohr drahr vee/kohm´•muhr vee frahm*
Is the flight delayed?	**Er flyet forsinket?**	*ar flui´•uh fohr•sihng´•kuht*
How late will it be?	**Hvor sent vil det bli?**	*voor sehnt vihl deh blee*

Luggage

Where is/are…?	**Hvor er…?**	*voor ar…*
the luggage carts [trolleys]	**bagasjetrallene**	*bah•gah´•shuh•trahl•luh•nuh*
the luggage lockers	**oppbevaringsboksene**	*ohp´•buh•vah•rihngs•bohk•su h•nuh*

the baggage claim	**bagasjeutleveringen**
	bah•gah´•shuh•ewt•leh•veh•ri hng•uhn
My luggage has been lost/stolen.	**Bagasjen min er tapt/stjålet.**
	bahg•ahsh•uhn mihn ar tahpt/stjawl•uht
My suitcase was damaged.	**Kofferten min ble skadet.**
	kuf´•fuhr•tuhn mihn bleh skah´•duht

Finding your Way

Where is...?	**Hvor er...?** *voor ar...*
the currency exchange office	**vekslingskontoret** <u>vehks</u>´•lihngs•kun•too•ruh
the exit	**utgangen** <u>ewt</u>´•gahng•uhn
the taxi stand [rank]	**drosjeholdeplassen** <u>drohsh</u>´•uh•hol•luh•plahs•suhn
the car hire	**bilutleie** beel•ewt•lay•eh
Is there... into town?	**Går det... inn til byen?** gawr deh... ihn tihl by•ehn
a bus	**en buss** ehn bews
a train	**et tog** eht tawg
an underground station	**En T-bane** ehn teh•bahn•eh

For Asking Directions, see page 34.

YOU MAY HEAR...

Ta plass. *tah plahs*	All aboard.
Billetter, takk. *bihl•<u>leht</u>´•tuhr tahk*	Tickets, please.
Du må bytte i... *dew maw <u>buit</u>´•tuh ih...*	You have to change at...
Neste holdeplass... *<u>nehs</u>´•tuh <u>hohl</u>´•luh•plahs...*	Next stop...

Norway runs a train network more than 4,000 km (c. 2,500 miles) long, though the system is much more comprehensive in the south than the north. Oslo is the main hub for most long-distance, express and local trains. Long-distance lines that span the country are an excellent way to view the incredible Norwegian scenery. A number of discounts are available: children under 4 travel free of charge, and children under 16 and senior citizens travel at half price. Local buses, trams, subways and ferries run on an integrated network, so you may transfer at no additional cost. Keep in mind that buying a **flexikort** (multi-trip ticket) is cheaper than buying single tickets. For moving around the capital, you may also want to consider a 1-, 2- or 3-day (children's or family) **Oslo Pass**, which offers unlimited public transportation within greater Oslo and free entry to a number of museums and tourist attractions. For long-distance travel, passes such as Eurorail (non-European residents), InterRail (European residents) or ScanRail (for travel within Scandinavia) can offer better value fares.

Train

How do I get to the train station?	**Hvordan kommer jeg til jernbanestasjonen?** _voor´·dahn kohm´·muhr yay tihl ya´rn·bah·nuh·stah·shoo·nuhn_
Is it far from here?	**Er det langt herfra?** _ar deh lahngt ha´r·frah_
Where is/are...?	**Hvor er...?** _voor ar..._
the ticket office	**billettluken** _bihl·leht´·lew·kuhn_
the information desk	**informasjonsskranken** _ihn·fohr·mah·shoo´ns·skrahng·kuhn_
the platforms	**perrongene** _par·awng·ehn·uh_
the luggage lockers	**bagasjeskapene** _bahg·ahsh·uh·skahp·ehn·uh_
Can I have a train schedule [timetable]?	**Kan jeg få en togtabell?** _kahn yay faw ehn tawg`·tah·behl_
How long is the trip?	**Hvor lang er turen?** _voor lang ar tew´·ruhn_
Is it a direct train?	**Går toget direkte?** _gawr tawg·eht deeh·rehk·teh_
Do I have to change trains?	**Må jeg bytte tog?** _maw yay buit`·tuh taw_
Is the train on time?	**Er toget i rute?** _ar tawg·eht ee rewt·eh_

For Tickets, see page 20.

Departures

Which track [platform] does the train to Skien leave from?	**Fra hvilket spor går toget til Skien?** _frah vihl´·kuht spoor gawr taw´·guh til sheh`·uhn_
Is this the track [platform] to...?	**Er dette sporet til...?** _ar deht`·tuh spoo´·ruh tihl..._
Where is track [platform]...?	**Hvor er spor...?** _voor ar spoor..._
Where do I change for...?	**Hvor må jeg bytte for å komme til...?** _voor maw yay buit`·tuh fohr aw kohm`·muh tihl..._

On Board

Is this seat taken?	**Er denne plassen opptatt?** _ar dehn`•nuh plahs´•suhn ohp´•taht_
Can I sit here?	**Kan jeg sitte her?** _kahn yay siht•uh har_
Can I open the window?	**Kan jeg åpne vinduet?** _kahn yay awpn•eh vihn•dew•eh_
I think that's my seat.	**Jeg tror at det er min plass.** _yay troor aht deh ar meen plahs_
Here's my reservation.	**Her er reservasjonen min.** _har ar rehs•ehr•vahsh•un•uhn mihn_

Bus

Where's the bus station?	**Hvor er busstasjonen?** _voor ar bews´•sta•shoo•nuhn_
How far is it?	**Hvor langt er det?** _voor lahngt ar deh_
How do I get to…?	**Hvordan kommer jeg til…?** _voor´•dahn kohm´• muhr yay tihl…_
Does the bus/train stop at (place/area)…?	**Stopper bussen/trikken (ved/på)…?** _stohp`•puhr bews´•suhn/trihk´•kuhn (veh/poh)…_
Can you tell me when to get off?	**Kan du si meg når jeg skal av?** _kahn dew see may nohr yay skahl ah_
Do I have to change buses?	**Må jeg bytte buss?** _maw yay buit`•tuh bews_

YOU MAY SEE...

BUSSHOLDEPLASS/ TRIKKEHOLDEPLASS	bus stop/train stop
STOPP	request stop
INNGANG/UTGANG	enter/exit
STEMPLE BILLETTEN	stamp your ticket

| Can you stop here? | **Kan du stoppe her?** *kahn dew stohp`•puh har* |

or Tickets, see page 20.

or Asking Directions, see page 34.

T-bane

Where's the nearest subway [underground] station?	**Hvor er nærmeste T-banestasjon?** *voor ar nar`•mehs•tuh teh`•bah•nuh•stah•shoon*
Can I have a map of the subway [underground]?	**Kan jeg få et kart over T-banen?** *kahn yay faw eht kart aw`•vuhr teh`•bah•nuh*
Which line for…?	**Hvilken linje går til…?** *vihl`•kuhn lihn`•yuh gawr tihl…*
Which direction?	**Hvilken retning?** *vee'k•ehn reht•nihng*
Where do I change for…?	**Hvor må jeg bytte for å komme til…?** *voor maw yay buit`•tuh fohr aw kohm`•muh tihl…*
Is this the right train for…?	**Er dette toget til…?** *ar deht`•tuh taw`•guh tihl…*
How many stops to…	**Hvor mange stoppesteder er det før…?** *voor mahn•geh stohp•puh•steh•duhr ar deh fur*
Where are we?	**Hvor er vi?** *voor ar vee*

or Tickets, see page 20.

The Oslo **Tunnelbane** or **T-bane** (subway) runs from approximately 5:30 a.m. to just after midnight. Buying a **flexikort** (multi-trip ticket) is a good idea if you plan on making numerous trips. It can be used to make transfers within one hour at no extra charge. An **Oslo Pass** is another discount travel pass, good for all forms of public transportation.

Boat & Ferry

When does the boat/ferry for…leave?	**Når går båten/fergen til…?** *nohr gawr baw´•tuhr fehr`•guhn tihl…*
Can I take my car?	**Kan jeg ta med bilen?** *kahn yay tah`•meh bee´•luh*
What time is the next sailing?	**Når er neste avgang?** *nawr ar nehs•tuh ahv•gahng*
Can I book a seat/cabin?	**Kan jeg bestille en plass/lugar?** *kahn yay behs•tihl•uh ehn plahs/lewg•ahr*
How long is the crossing?	**Hvor lang er overfarten?** *voor lahng ar awv•ehr•fahrt•ehn*

For Tickets, see page 20.

Ferry and boat travel is efficient in Norway. Most ferries and high-speed ships have frequent departure schedules, so you rarely have to wait in lines, and the cost for passenger and car transport is generally low. Besides regular ferry service, several companies offer cruises along the fjords. These are very popular during the summer months and tickets are more expensive during this period, so reservations should be made well in advance.

Taxi

Where can I get a taxi?	**Hvor kan jeg få tak i en drosje?** *voor kahn yay faw tahk ih ehn droh`•shuh*
I'd like a taxi now/for tomorrow at…	**Jeg trenger en drosje nå/i morgen klokken…** *yay trehng´•uhr ehn droh`•shuh naw/ih mawr`•uhn klohk`•kuhn…*
Can you pick me up…?	**Kan du hente meg…?** *kahn dew hehn`•tuh may.*
at the airport	**på flyplassen** *poh flui´•plahs•suhn*
at the ferry landing	**ved fergeleiet** *veh fer`•guh•lay•uh*
at eight o'clock	**klokken åtte** *klohk`•kuhn oht`•tuh*

Take me to...	**Kjør meg til...** *khurr may tihl...*	
this address	**denne adressen** <u>*dehn`*</u>*·nuh ahd·*<u>*rehs´*</u>*·suhn*	
the airport	**flyplassen** <u>*flui´*</u>*·plahs·suhn*	
the train station	**jernbanestasjonen** <u>*ya`rn*</u>*·bah·nuh·stah·shoon·uhn*	
I'm in a hurry.	**Jeg har dårlig tid.** *yay* <u>*hahr*</u> *dawr`·lih teed*	
Can you drive faster/ slower?	**Kan du kjøre fortere/saktere?** *kahn dew* <u>*khur`*</u>*·ruh* <u>*fohr`*</u>*·tuh·ruh/*<u>*sahk`*</u>*·tuh·ruh*	

Taxis can be hailed in the street, found at taxi stands or ordered by phone. All cabs are metered and service charges are included in the fare. You can tip the driver by rounding up the fare. Keep in mind that rates differ from place to place and travel by taxi is generally expensive, so ask for an approximate fare beforehand. Most taxis accept credit cards but be sure to double check first.

YOU MAY HEAR...

Hvor skal du? *voor* <u>*skahl*</u> *dew*	Where to?
Hva var adressen? *vah vahr ahd·*<u>*rehs´*</u>*·suhn*	What's the address?

Stop/Wait here.	**Stopp/Vent her.** *stohp/vehnt har*
How much?	**Hvor mye koster det?** *voor mui`·uh kohs`·tuhr deh*
You said…crowns.	**Du sa…kroner.** *dew sah…kroo`·nuhr*
Can I have a receipt?	**Kan jeg få en kvittering?** *kahn yay faw ehn kviht·teh´·rihng*
Keep the change.	**Behold vekslepengene.** *buh·hohl´ vehk`s·luh·pehng·uh·nuh*

Bicycle & Motorbike

I'd like to rent [hire]…	**Jeg vil gjerne leie…** *yay vihl ya`r·nuh lay`·uh…*
a bicycle	**en sykkel** *ehn suik´·kuhl*
a moped	**en moped** *ehn mu·peh´d*
a motorcycle	**en motorsykkel** *ehn moo´·toor·suik·kuhl*
How much per day/week?	**Hvor mye koster det per dag/uke?** *voor mui`·uh kohs`·tuhr deh pehr dahg/ew`·kuh*
Can I have a helmet/lock?	**Kan jeg få med hjelm/lås?** *kahn yay faw`·meh yehlm/laws*

Car Hire

If you enjoy cycling there are many well-planned routes throughout the country, through lush valleys and breathtaking fjords. Attractions are usually signposted. You can bring your own bike or rent one easily. Given the terrain, a **terrengsykkel** (mountain bike) is usually the most practical option.

Where can I rent a car?	**Hvor kan jeg leie en bil?** *voor kahn yay lay`·uh ehn beel*
I'd like to rent [hire]…	**Jeg vil gjerne leie…** *yay vihl ya`r·nuh lay`·uh…*
a 2-/4-door car	**en to-dørs/firedørs bil** *ehn too´·durrs/fee´·ruh·durrs beel*
an automatic	**en bil med automatgir** *meh ev·tu·mah´t·geer*

a car with air conditioning	**en bil med klimaanlegg** *ehn b**eel** meh kl**ee**´·mah·ahn·lehg*
a car seat	**et barnesete** *eht b**ahr**`·nuh·seh·tuh*
a cheap/small car	**en billig/liten bil** *ehn bihl·ih/liht·ehn beel*
How much…?	**Hvor mye koster det…?** *voor m**ui**`·uh k**ohs**´·tuhr deh…*

YOU MAY HEAR…

Har du et internasjonalt førerkort? *h**ahr** d**ew** eht ihn´·tuhr·nah·shu·n**ah**lt f**ur**`·ruhr·kohrt*	Do you have an international driver's license?
Kan jeg få se passet? *kahn yay faw seh pahs*´·suh*	Can I see your passport?
Vil du ha forsikring? *vihl dew hah fohr·s**ihk**´·rihng*	Do you want insurance?
Det er et depositum på… *deh ar eht deh·p**oo**´·sih·tewm poh…*	There is a deposit of…
Undertegn her. *ewn*`·nuhr·tayn h**ar***	Please sign here.

per day	**per dag** *pehr d**ah**g*
per week	**per uke** *pehr **ew**`·kuh*
per kilometer	**per kilometer** *pehr kh**ee**´·lu·meh·tuhr*
for unlimited mileage	**for ubegrenset kjørelengde** *fohr **ew**`·buh·grehn·suht kh**ur**`·ruh·lehng·duh*
with insurance	**inkludert forsikring** *ihn·klew·d**ehr**´ fohr·s**ihk**´·rihng*
Are there any discounts?	**Er det noen rabatter?** *ar deh n**oo**`·uhn rah·b**aht**´·tuhr*

Fuel Station

Where's the nearest gas [petrol] station?	**Hvor er nærmeste bensinstasjon?** *voor ar ner`•mehs•tuh behn•<u>seen</u>´•stah•sho<u>on</u>*
Fill it up, please.	**Full tank, takk.** *fewl tahngk tahk*
…liters, please.	**…liter bensin, takk.** *…<u>lee</u>´•tuhr behn•<u>seen</u>´ tahk*
Can I pay in cash/by credit card?	**Kan jeg betale kontant/med kredittkort?** *kahn y buh•<u>tah</u>´•luh kun•<u>tahn</u>´t /meh <u>kreh</u>•diht´•<u>kohrt</u>*

YOU MAY SEE...

NORMAL 95 OKTAN	regular
SUPER 98 OKTAN	premium [super]
DIESEL	diesel

Asking Directions

Are we on the right road for…?	**Er dette veien til…?** *ar deht`•tuh <u>vay</u>´•uhn tihl…*
How far is it to…?	**Hvor langt er det til…?** *<u>voor lahngt</u> <u>a</u>r deh tihl…*
Where's…?	**Hvor er…?** *voor ar…*
…Street	**…gate** *…<u>gah</u>`•tuh*
this address	**denne adressen** *<u>dehn</u>`•nuh ahd•<u>rehs</u>´•suhn*

YOU MAY HEAR...

rett frem *reht frehm*	straight ahead
på venstre side *poh vehn´•struh see`•duh*	on the left
på høyre side *poh hury´•ruh see`•duh*	on the right
på/rundt hjørnet *poh/rewnt yurr`•nuh*	on/around the corner
midt imot... *miht ih•moot´...*	opposite...
bak... *bahk...*	behind...
ved siden av... *veh see`•duhn ah...*	next to...
etter... *eht`•tuhr...*	after...
nord/sør *noor/surr*	north/south
øst/vest *urst/vehst*	east/west
ved lyskrysset *veh lui`s•kruis•suh*	at the traffic light
ved veikrysset *veh vay`•kruis•suh*	at the intersection

the highway [motorway]	**motorveien** *moo´•toor•vay•uhn*
Can you show me where I am on the map?	**Kan du vise meg på kartet hvor jeg er?** *kahn dew vee`•suh may paw kahr´•tuh voor yay ar*
I'm lost.	**Jeg har gått meg vill.** *yay hahr goht may vihl*

Parking

Can I park here?	**Kan jeg parkere her?** *kahn yay pahr•keh´•ruh har*
Is there a parking lot [car park] nearby?	**Fins det en parkeringsplass i nærheten?** *fins deh ehn pahr•keh´•rihngs•plahs ih nar´•heh•tuhn*
How much...?	**Hvor mye koster det...?** *voor mui`•uh kohs`•tuhr deh...*
per hour	**per time** *pehr tee`•muh*
per day	**per dag** *pehr dahg*
for overnight	**over natten** *aw´•vuhr naht´•tuhn*

Parking in Norway is restricted, particularly on weekdays. The most common system is the **P-automat** (automated parking meter) when you park your car, then pay for an amount of time at the meter; the meter then prints a ticket to be displayed on your dashboard. Another option is a **P-hus** (parking garage) when you receive a ticket upon entering the garage. Before getting into your car to leave the garage, you must pay for your ticket at an automated machine or a manned booth.

YOU MAY SEE...

STOP	**STOPP**	stop
	VIKEPLIKT	yield
	PARKERING FORBUDT	no parking
	ÉNVEISKJØRING	one way
	INNKJØRING FORBUDT	no entry
	FORBIKJØRING FORBUDT	no passing
	U-SVING FORBUDT	no U-turn
	GANGFELT	pedestrian crossing

Breakdown & Repair

My car broke down/ won't start.	**Bilen har fått motorstopp/starter ikke.** _bee´-luhn_ _hahr foht moo´-toor-stohp/ stahr`-tuhr ihk`-kuh_
Can you fix it (today)?	**Kan du reparere den i dag?** _kahn dew reh-pah-reh´-ruh dehn ee dahg_
When will it be ready?	**Når er den klar?** _nohr ar dehn klahr_
How much?	**Hvor mye koster det?** _voor mui`-uh kohs`-tuhr deh_
I have a puncture/ flat tyre	**Jeg har punktert/et flatt dekk** _yay hahr punk-tehrt/ eht flaht dehk_

Accidents

There's been an accident.	**Det har skjedd en ulykke.** _deh hahr shehd ehn ew`-lui-kuh_
Call a doctor/an ambulance!	**Ring etter lege/sykebil!** _rihng eht`-tuhr leh`-guh/ sui`-kuh-beel_

Places to Stay

ESSENTIAL

Can you recommend a hotel?	**Kan du anbefale et hotell?** *kahn dew ahn´•buh•fah•luh eht hu•tehl´*
I have a reservation.	**Jeg har bestilt rom.** *yay hahr buh•stihlt´ rum*
My name is…	**Jeg heter…** *yay heh´•tuhr…*
Do you have a room…?	**Har dere et rom…?** *hahr deh`•ruh eht rum…*
for one/two	**for én/to** *fohr ehn/too*
with a bathroom	**med bad** *meh bahd*
with air conditioning	**med klimaanlegg** *meh klee´•mah•ahn•lehg*
For tonight.	**For i natt.** *fohr ih naht*
For two nights.	**For to netter.** *fohr too neht´•tuhr*
For one week.	**For en uke.** *fohr ehn ew`•kuh*
How much?	**Hvor mye koster det?** *voor mui´•uh kohs´•tuhr deh*
Do you have anything cheaper?	**Har dere noe rimeligere?** *hahr deh`•ruh noo`•uh ree`•muh•lih•uh•ruh*
When's check-out?	**Når må jeg sjekke ut?** *nohr maw yay shehk´•kuh ewt*
Can I leave this in the safe?	**Kan jeg legge denne/dette igjen i safen?** *kahn yay lehg`•guh dehn`•nuh/deht`•tuh ih•yehn´ ih sayf´•uhn*
Can I leave my bags?	**Kan jeg sette igjen bagasjen?** *kahn yay seht`•tuh ih•yehn´ bah•gah´•shuhn*
Can I have the bill/ a receipt?	**Kan jeg få regningen/en kvittering?** *kahn yay faw ray`•ning•uhn/ehn kviht•teh´•rihng*
I'll pay in cash/by credit card.	**Jeg betaler kontant/med kredittkort.** *yay buh•tah´•luhr kun•tahnt´/meh kreh•diht´•kohrt*

In Norway, there are a variety of accommodation alternatives
in addition to more conventional options such as hotels, bed and
breakfasts or **husrom** (rooms in private houses) and **vandrerhjem**
(hostels). For a unique holiday experience you could consider a
bondegårdsferie (farm stay), which lets you taste Norwegian farm
life firsthand. Similarly, along the coast, you could arrange to stay in
rorbuer (fisherman's cabins). **Hytter** (chalets or cabins) are available
throughout the country as well.

Somewhere to Stay

Can you recommend…?	**Kan du anbefale…?**	kahn dew <u>ahn</u>´·buh·**fah**·luh
a bed and breakfast	**et rom inklusive frokost?**	eht rum ihnk·lews·ihv·eh fru·kawst
a campsite	**en campingplass?**	ehn kamp·ihng·plahs
a hostel	**et hospits?**	eht hus·pihts
a hotel	**et hotel**	eht hu·tehl´
What is it near?	**Hva er det i nærheten?**	vah <u>a</u>r deh ih <u>nar</u>´·**heh**·tuhn
How do I get there?	**Hvordan kommer jeg dit?**	<u>voor</u>´·dahn kohm´·muhr yay d**ee**t

If you didn't reserve a room before your arrival, the local
tourist office can provide information and help you to arrange
a reservation. The official website of the Norwegian Tourist Board,
Visit Norway (www.visitnorway.com), can provide information about
locations in particular cities.

At the Hotel

I have a reservation.	**Jeg har bestilt rom.**	*yay hahr buh•stihlt´ rum*
My name is…	**Jeg heter…**	*yay heh`•tuhr…*
Do you have a room…?	**Har dere et rom…?**	*hahr deh`•ruh eht rum…*
with a bathroom/ shower	**med bad/dusj**	*meh bahd/dewsh*
with a private toilet	**med toalett**	*meh tu•ah•leht*
with air conditioning	**med klimaanlegg**	*meh klee´•mah•ahn•lehg*
that's smoking/ non-smoking	**for røykere/ikke-røykere**	*fohr ruryk`•uh•ruh/ ihk`•kuh•ruryk•uhr•uh*
For…	**For…**	*fawr*
tonight	**i natt**	*ee naht*
two nights	**to netter**	*tu neht•ehr*
a week	**en uke**	*ehn ewk•eh*
Can I access the internet?	**Kan jeg bruke internett?**	*kahn yay brew´•kuh ihn´•tuhr•neht*
Does the hotel have…?	**Har hotellet…?**	*hahr hu•tehl´•uh…*
a computer	**en datamaskin**	*ehn dah´•tah•mah•sheen*

Norwegian electricity is generally 220 volts and round two-pin plugs are typically used. British and American appliances may need an adapter.

(wireless) internet service	**(trådløst) Internett**	trawd•lurst ihnt•ar•neht
an elevator [lift]	**heis**	hays
room service	**romservice**	rum`•sur•vihs
a gym	**trimrom**	trihm´•rum
a pool	**et basseng**	eht bahs•ehng
I need...	**Jeg trenger...**	yay trehng´•uhr...
an extra bed	**en ekstra seng**	ehn ehks´•trah sehng
a cot [camp bed]	**en feltseng**	ehn fehlt´•sehng
a crib [child's cot]	**en barneseng**	ehn bahr`•nuh•sehng

YOU MAY SEE...

SKYV/TREKK	push/pull
TOALETT	restroom [toilet]
DUSJ	shower
HEIS	elevator [lift]
TRAPP	stairs
VAREAUTOMATER	vending machines
IS	ice
VASKERI	laundry
IKKE FORSTYRR	do not disturb
BRANNDØR	fire door
NØDUTGANG	emergency/fire exit
VEKKING	wake-up call

Price

How much per night/week?	**Hvor mye koster det per natt/uke?** *voor <u>mui</u>`•uh <u>kohs</u>`•tuhr deh pehr naht/<u>ew</u>`•kuh*
Does the price include breakfast/sales tax [VAT]?	**Er frokost/moms inkludert i prisen?** *ar <u>froo</u>´•kust mums ihn•klu•<u>dehrt</u>´ ih <u>pree</u>´•suhn*
Are there any discounts?	**Har dere noen rabatter?** *hahr dehr•eh nu•ehn rah•baht•ehr*

Preferences

Can I see the room?	**Kan jeg få se rommet?** *kahn yay faw seh paw rum•eht*
I'd like a…room.	**Jeg vil gjerne ha et…rom.** *yay vihl yar•neh hah eht rum*
better	**bedre** *beh•dreh*
bigger	**større** *stur•reh*
cheaper	**billigere** *bihl•ihg•ehr•eh*
quieter	**roligere** *ru•lihg•ehr•eh*
I'll take it.	**Jeg tar det.** *yay tahr deh*
No, I won't take it.	**Nei, jeg vil ikke ha det.** *nai, yay vihl ihk•eh hah deh*

Questions

Where's…?	**Hvor er…?** *voor ar…*
the bar	**baren** *<u>bah</u>´•ruhn*
the bathroom	**toalettet** *tu•ah•<u>leht</u>´•uh*
the elevator [lift]	**heisen** *<u>hay</u>´•suhn*
Can I have…?	**Kan jeg få…?** *kahn yay faw…*
a blanket	**et ullteppe** *eht <u>ewl</u>`•tehp•puh*
an iron	**et strykejern** *eht <u>strui</u>`•kuh•yarn*
a pillow	**en pute** *ehn <u>pew</u>`•tuh*
the room key/key card	**romnøkkelen/nøkkelkortet?** *rum•nurk•ehl•ehn/nurk•ehl•kurt•eht*

a soap	**en såpe** ehn <u>saw</u>`-puh
toilet paper	**toalettpapir** tu-ah-<u>leht</u>´-pah-peer
a towel	**et håndkle** eht <u>hohng</u>`-kleh
Do you have an adapter for this?	**Har du en adapter til denne/dette?** <u>hahr</u> dew ehn ahd-<u>ahp</u>´-tuhr tihl <u>dehn</u>`-nuh/<u>deht</u>`-tuh
How do I turn on the lights?	**Hvordan slår jeg på lyset?** <u>voor</u>´-dahn slawr yay poh <u>lui</u>´s-uh
Can you wake me at…?	**Kan du vekke meg klokken…?** kahn dew <u>vehk</u>`-kuh may <u>klohk</u>`-kuhn…
Can I leave this in the safe?	**Kan jeg få legge denne i safen?** kahn yay faw <u>lehg</u>-eh dehn-eh ee sayf-ehn
Could I have my things from the safe?	**Kan jeg få sakene mine fra safen?** kahn yay faw <u>sah</u>`-kuh-nuh <u>mee</u>`-nuh frah <u>say</u>´-fuhn
Is/are there any mail/messages for me?	**Har det kommet noe post/noen beskjed til meg?** hahr deh <u>kohm</u>`-muht <u>noo</u>`-uh pohst/<u>noo</u>`-uhn buh-<u>sheh</u>´ tihl may
Do you have a laundry service?	**Har dere vaskeritjenester?** hahr dehr-uh vahsk-ehr-ee-tjehn-ehst-uhr

YOU MAY HEAR…

Passet/kredittkortet ditt, takk. <u>pah</u>´-suh/kreh-<u>diht</u>´-kohr-tuh diht tahk — Your passport/credit card, please.

Kan du fylle ut dette skjemaet? kahn dew <u>fui</u>`-luh ewt <u>deht</u>´-tuh <u>sheh</u>´-mah-uh — Can you fill out this form?

Undertegn her. <u>ewn</u>`-nuhr-tayn har — Sign here.

Problems

| There's a problem. | **Jeg har et problem.** yay hahr eht pru-<u>bleh</u>´m |
| I've lost my key/key card. | **Jeg har mistet nøkkelen/nøkkelkortet.** yay hahr <u>mihs</u>`-tuht <u>nurk</u>`-kehl-uhn/<u>nurk</u>`-kehl-kor-tuh |

I've locked myself out of my room.	**Jeg har låst meg ute fra rommet.** *yay hahr lawst may ew`•tuh fra rum´•muh*
There's no hot water/ toilet paper.	**Jeg har ikke varmt vann/toalettpapir.** *yay hahr ihk`•kuh vahrmt vahn/tu•ah•leht´•pah•peer*
The room is dirty.	**Rommet er skittent** *rum´•muh ar shiht´•tuhnt*
There are bugs in our room.	**Det er insekter på rommet vårt.** *deh ar ihn`•sehk•tuhr poh rum´•muh vohrt*
…doesn't work.	**…virker ikke.** *…vihr`•kuhr ihk`•kuh*
Can you fix…?	**Kan du få fikset…?** *kahn dew faw fihk`•suht…*
the air conditioning	**klimaanlegget** *klee´•mah•ahn•lehg•guh*
the fan	**viften** *vihf´•tuhn*
the heat [heating]	**varmen** *vahr´•muhn*
the light	**lyset** *lui´s•uh*
the TV	**TVen** *teh`•veh•uhn*
the toilet	**toalettet** *tu•ah•leht´•tuh*
I'd like to move to another room.	**Jeg vil gjerne flytte til et annet rom.** *yay vihl ya`r•nuh fluit´•tuh tihl eht ahn`•nuht rum*

Checking Out

| When's check-out? | **Når må jeg sjekke ut?** *nohr maw yay shehk`•kuh ew* |
| Could I leave my bags here until…? | **Kan jeg sette igjen bagasjen min til…?** *kahn yay seht`•tuh ih•yehn´ bah•gah´•shuhn mihn tihl…* |

Can I have an itemized bill/a receipt?	**Kan jeg få en spesifisert regning/kvittering?** *kahn yay faw ehn speh·sih·fih·<u>sehrt´</u> <u>ray`</u>·ning/ kviht·<u>teh´</u>·rihng*
I think there's a mistake in the bill.	**Jeg tror det er en feil på regningen.** *yay <u>troor</u> deh ar ehn fayl poh <u>ray`</u>·ning·uhn*
I'll pay in cash/by credit card.	**Jeg betaler kontant/med kredittkort.** *yay buh·<u>tah´</u>·luhr kun·<u>tahnt´</u>/meh <u>kreh</u>·diht´·kohrt*

For Grammar, see page 165.

Renting

I've reserved an apartment/a room.	**Jeg har bestilt leilighet/rom.** *yay hahr buh·<u>stihlt´</u> <u>lay`</u>·li·h<u>eh</u>t/rum*
My name is...	**Jeg heter...** *yay <u>heh´</u>·tuhr...*
Can I have the key/ key card?	**Kan jeg få nøkkelen/nøkkelkortet?** *kahn yay faw <u>nurk`</u>·kuhl·uhn/ <u>nurk`</u>·kuhl·kor·tuh*
Are there...?	**Fins det...?** *fihns deh...*
dishes	**servise** *sehr·<u>vee´</u>·suh*
pillows	**puter** <u>pew`</u>·tuhr
sheets	**lakener** <u>lah´</u>·kuhn·uhr
towels	**håndklær** <u>hohng`</u>·klar
When/Where do I put out the trash [rubbish] recycling?	**Når/Hvor setter jeg ut søppelet?** *nohr/voor <u>seht´</u>·tuhr yay <u>ewt</u> surp´·puhl·uh*
...is broken.	**...er gått i stykker.** *...ar goht ih <u>stuik´</u>·kuhr*
How does...work?	**Hvordan virker...?** <u>voor´</u>·dahn <u>vihr´</u>·kuhr
the air conditioner	**klimaanlegget** <u>klee´</u>·mah·ahn·lehg·guh
the dishwasher	**oppvaskmaskinen** <u>ohp`</u>·vahsk·mah·sheen·uhn
the freezer	**fryseren** <u>frui`</u>·suhr·uhn
the heater	**varmeovnen** <u>vahr´</u>·muh·ohv·nuhn
the microwave	**mikrobølgeovnen** <u>mih´</u>·kru·burl·guh·ohv·nuhn
the refrigerator	**kjøleskapet** <u>khur`</u>·luh·skahpuh

| the stove | **komfyren** kohm·<u>fui</u>´·ruhn |
| the washing machine | **vaskemaskinen** <u>vahs</u>`·kuh·mah·sheen·uhn |

Domestic Items

I need…	**Jeg trenger…** yay <u>trehng</u>´·uhr…
an adapter	**en adapter** ehn ah·<u>dahp</u>´·tuhr
aluminum [kitchen] foil	**aluminiumsfolie** ah·lew·<u>meen</u>´·yewms·fool·yuh
a bottle opener	**en flaskeåpner** ehn <u>flahs</u>`·kuh·awp·nuhr
a broom	**en feiekost** ehn <u>fay</u>`·uh·kust
a can opener	**en boksåpner** ehn <u>bohks</u>`·awp·nuhr
cleaning supplies	**rengjøringsmidler** <u>rehn</u>`·yurr·ihngs·mihd·luhr
a corkscrew	**en korketrekker** ehn <u>kohr</u>`·kuh·trehk·kuhr
detergent	**vaskemiddel** <u>vahs</u>`·kuh·mihd·duhl
dish detergent	**oppvaskmiddel** <u>ohp</u>`·vahsk·mid·duhl
bin bags	**søppelsekker** <u>surp</u>`·puhl·sehk·kuhr
a light bulb	**en lyspære** ehn <u>lui</u>`s·pa·ruh
matches	**fyrstikker** <u>fuir</u>`·stihk·kuhr
a mop	**en mopp** ehn mawp
a napkin	**en serviett** ehn sehrv·<u>yeht</u>´
paper towels	**husholdningspapir** hews·<u>hohl</u>´·nihngs·pah·peer
plastic wrap [cling film]	**plastfolie** <u>plahst</u>´·fool·yuh
a plunger	**en klosettpumpe** ehn klu·seht´·pum·puh
scissors	**en saks** ehn sahks
a vacuum cleaner	**en støvsuger** ehn <u>stur</u>`v·sewg·uhr

At the Hostel

| Do you have any places left for tonight? | **Har dere noen plasser ledig for i natt?** hahr <u>deh</u>`·ruh <u>noo</u>`·uhn plahs`·suhr <u>leh</u>`·dih fohr ih naht |

Can I have…?	**Kan jeg få…?** *kahn yay faw*…
a single/double room	**et enkeltrom/dobbeltrom** *eht <u>ehng</u>´·kuhlt·rum/ <u>dohb</u>´·buhlt·rum*
a blanket	**et ullteppe** *eht <u>ewl</u>´·tehp·puh*
a pillow	**en pute** *ehn <u>pew</u>`·tuh*
some sheets	**noe sengetøy** *nu·eh sehng·eh·tury*
soap	**såpe** *<u>saw</u>´·puh*
towels	**håndklær** *<u>hohng</u>`·klar*
What time do you lock up?	**Når stenges ytterdøra?** *nohr <u>stehng</u>`·uhs <u>uit</u>`·tuhr·**dur**·rah*

There are well over 100 hostels throughout Norway run by two different chains: Hostelling International, monitored by **Norske Vandrerhjem** (the Norwegian branch of Hostelling International), and VIP Backpackers Resorts International. Located in cities as well as natural settings like fjords and along the coast, hostels are an inexpensive option. In many cases you may request a private or shared room. The charge per night covers only the cost of the room. Sheets may be brought from home or rented, and meals are separate.

Going Camping

Can we camp here?	**Kan vi campe her?** *kahn vee <u>kehm</u>`·puh har*	
Is there a campsite nearby?	**Er det en campingplass i nærheten?** *<u>a</u>r deh ehn <u>kehm</u>´·pihng·plahs ih <u>nar</u>´·heh·tuhn*	
What is the charge per day/week?	**Hva koster det per dag/uke?** *vah <u>kohs</u>`·tuhr deh pehr dahg/<u>ew</u>`·kuh*	
Are there…?	**Fins det…?** *fihns deh…*	
cooking facilities	**kokemuligheter** *<u>koo</u>`·kuh·<u>mew</u>·lih·heht·uhr*	
electrical outlets	**innlagt strøm** *<u>ihn</u>´·lahkt strurm*	
laundry facilities	**vaskemuligheter** *<u>vahs</u>`·kuh·<u>mew</u>·lih·heht·uhr*	
showers	**dusj** *dewsh*	
tents for rent [hire]	**telt til leie** *tehlt tihl <u>lay</u>`·uh*	
Where can I empty the chemical toilet?	**Hvor kan jeg tømme det kjemiske toalettet?** *vo kahn yay <u>turm</u>`·muh de <u>kheh</u>´·mihs·kuh tu·ah·<u>leht</u>·*	

YOU MAY SEE…

DRIKKEVANN	drinking water
CAMPING FORBUDT	no camping
BRUK AV ÅPEN ILD FORBUDT	no fires
GRILLING FORBUDT	no barbecues

ESSENTIAL

Where's an internet cafe?	**Hvor finner jeg en internettkafé?** *voor* <u>*fihn*</u>` *·nuhr yay ehn* <u>*ihn*</u>`*·tuhr·neht·kah·feh*
Can I access the internet/check e-mail?	**Kan jeg bruke internett/sjekke e-post?** *kahn yay* <u>*brew*</u>`*·kuh* <u>*ihn*</u>`*·tuhr·neht/*<u>*shehk*</u>`*·kuh* <u>**eh**</u>`*·pohst*
How much per hour/half hour?	**Hvor mye er det for en time/halv time?** *voor* <u>*mui*</u>`*·uh* <u>*ar*</u> *deh fohr ehn* <u>*tee*</u>`*·muh/hahl* <u>*tee*</u>`*·muh*
How do I connect/log on?	**Hvordan kobler jeg meg opp/logger jeg meg inn?** <u>*voor*</u>`*·dahn* <u>*kohb*</u>`*·luhr yay may ohp/*<u>*lohg*</u>`*·guhr yay may ihn*
Can I have a phone card?	**Kan jeg få et telefonkort?** *kahn yay faw eht teh·luh·*<u>**foon**</u>`*·kohrt*
Can I have your phone number?	**Kan jeg få telefonnummeret ditt?** *kahn yay faw teh·luh·*<u>**foon**</u>`*·num·muhr·uh diht*
Here's my number/e-mail address.	**Her har du nummeret mitt/ e-postadressen min.** *har* <u>*hahr*</u> *dew* <u>*num*</u>`*·muhr·uh miht/*<u>**eh**</u>`*·pohst·ahd·rehs·suhn mihn*
Call me.	**Ring meg.** *rihng may*
E-mail me.	**Send meg en e-post.** *sehn may ehn* <u>**eh**</u>`*·pohst*
Hello. This is…	**Hallo. Dette er…** *hah·*<u>*loo*</u>` *deht*`*·tuh ar…*
I'd like to speak to…	**Kan jeg få snakke med…?** *kahn yay faw* <u>*snahk*</u>`*·kuh meh…*
Can you repeat that?	**Kan du gjenta det?** *kahn dew* <u>*yehn*</u>`*·tah deh*
I'll call back later.	**Jeg ringer igjen senere.** *yay* <u>*rihng*</u>`*·uhr ih·*<u>*yehn*</u>` *seh*`*·nuh·ruh*
Goodbye.	**Adjø.** *ahd·*<u>*yur*</u>`
Where's the post office?	**Hvor er postkontoret?** *voor ar* <u>*pohst*</u>`*·kun·toor·uh*
Can I send this to…?	**Kan jeg få sendt dette til…?** *kahn yay faw sehnt* <u>*deht*</u>`*·tuh tihl…*

Online

Where's an internet cafe?	**Hvor finner jeg en internettkafé?** *voor fihn´·nuhr yay ehn ihn´·tuhr·neht·kah·feh*
Does it have wireless internet?	**Har den trådløst internett?** *hahr dehn traw`·lurst ihn´·tuhr·neht*
What is the WiFi password?	**Hva er WiFi-passordet?** *vah ar vee·fee·pahs·ur·eht*
Is the WiFi free?	**Er WiFi gratis?** *ar vee·fee grah·tihs*
Do you have bluetooth?	**Har dere bluetooth?** *hahr dehr·eh blew·tewth*
How do I turn the computer on/off?	**Hvordan slår jeg på/av datamaskinen?** *voor´·da slawr yay paw/ah dah´·tah·mah·sheen·uhn*
Can I...?	**Kan jeg...?** *kahn yay...*
access the Internet	**bruke internett** *brew`·kuh ihn´·tuhr·neht*
check e-mail	**sjekke e-post** *shehk`·kuh eh´·pohst*
print	**skrive ut** *skree`·vuh ewt*
plug in/charge my laptop/iPhone/ iPad/BlackBerry?	**koble til/lade min bærbare maskin/ iPhone/iPad BlackBerry?** *kawb·leh tihl/lah·deh mihn bar·bahr·eh mah·sheen/ay·foan/ay·pad/blahk·behr·ree*
access Skype?	**bruke Skype** *brew·keh skayp*
How much per hour/ half hour?	**Hvor mye er det for en time/halv time?** *voor mui`·uh ar deh fohr ehn tee`·muh/hahl tee´·muh*
How do I...?	**Hvordan...?** *voor´·dahn...*
connect/disconnect	**kobler jeg meg opp/fra** *kohb`·luhr yay may ohp/fr...*
log on/off	**logger jeg meg inn/ut** *lohg`·guhr jay may ihn/ewt*
type this symbol	**skriver jeg dette tegnet** *skree´·vuhr yay deht`·tuh tay´·nuh*
What's your e-mail?	**Hva er e-postadressen din?** *vah ar eh´·pohst·ahd·rehs·suhn dihn*
My e-mail is...	**E-postadressen min er...** *eh´·pohst·ahd·rehs·suh mihn ar...*
Do you have a scanner?	**Har dere en skanner?** *hahr dehr·eh ehn skahn·ehr*

YOU MAY SEE...

LUKK	close
SLETT	delete
E-POST	e-mail
AVSLUTT	exit
HJELP	help
INSTANT MESSENGER	instant messenger
INTERNETT	internet
PÅLOGGING	log in
NY (MELDING)	new (message)
PÅ/AV	on/off
ÅPNE	open
SKRIV UT	print
LAGRE	save
SEND	send
BRUKERNAVN/PASSORD	username/password
TRÅDLØST INTERNETT	wireless internet

Social Media

Are you on Facebook/ Twitter?	**Er du på Facebook/Twitter?**	*ar dew paw feis•bewk/ tviht•ehr*
What's your user name?	**Hva er brukernavnet ditt?**	*vah ar brewk•ehr•nahvn•eht diht*
I'll add you as a friend.	**Jeg legger deg til som venn.**	*yay lehg•ehr day tihl sawm vehn*
I'll follow you on Twitter.	**Jeg følger deg på Twitter.**	*yay furl•ehr day paw tviht•ehr*
Are you following...?	**Følger du...?**	*furl•her dew*
I'll put the pictures on Facebook/Twitter.	**Jeg legger ut bildene på Facebook/Twitter.**	*yay lehg•ehr ewt bihl•deh•neh paw feis•bewk/tviht•ehr*

| I'll tag you in the pictures. | **Jeg tagger deg i bildene.** yay tag•ehr day ee bihl•dehn•eh |

Phone

Can I have a phone card/prepaid calling time for… crowns?	**Kan jeg få et telefonkort/ringetid for… kroner?** kahn yay faw eht teh•luh•_foon_´•kohrt/_rihng_`•uh•_teed_ fohr… _kroo_`n•uhr
How much?	**Hvor mye koster det?** voor _mui_´•uh kohs`•tuhr deh
Where's the pay phone?	**Hvor er telefonautomaten?** voor ar teh•leh•fun•ev•tu•maht•ehn
What's the area/country code for…?	**Hva er retningsnummeret/landkoden til…?** vah ar _reht_`•nihngs•num•muhr•uh/_lahn_`•_kood_•uhn tihl…
What's the number for Information?	**Hva er nummeret til Opplysningen?** vah ar _num_´•muhr•uh tihl ohp•_luis_´•nihng•uhn
Can I have the number for…?	**Kan jeg få nummeret til…?** kahn yay faw _num_´•muhr•uh tihl…
I'd like to call collect [reverse the charges].	**Jeg vil ringe med noteringsoverføring [mottaker betaler].** yay vihl rihn•geh meh nut•ehr•ihngs•awv•ehr•furr•ihng mut•ahk•ehr beh•tah•lehr
My cell [mobile] phone doesn't work here.	**Mobilen min virker ikke her.** mu•_beel_´•uhn mihn _vihr_`•kuhr _ihk_`•kuh har

---

In Norway, public phones accept coins, credit cards or **telekort** (prepaid phone cards), which are available at most kiosks, post offices and major train stations.

To call the U.S. or Canada from Norway, dial 00 + 1 + area code + phone number. To call the U.K., dial 00 + 44 + area code (minus the first 0) + phone number. Useful numbers include: information **1880**; operator assistance **1882**.

What network are you on?	**Hvilket nettverk er du på?** *vihl•keht neht•vahrk ar dew paw*	
Is it 3G?	**Er det 3G?** *ar deh treh•geh*	
I have run out of credit/minutes.	**Jeg gikk tom for kreditt/minutter.** *yay yihk tawm fawr kreh•diht/mihn•ewt•ehr*	
Can I buy some credit?	**Kan jeg kjøpe litt kreditt?** *kahn yay shur•peh liht kreh•diht*	
Do you have a phone charger?	**Har du en telefonlader?** *Hahr dew ehn teh•leh•fun•lah•dehr*	

YOU MAY HEAR...

Hvem er det som ringer? *vehm ar deh sohm rihng`•uhr*	Who's calling?
Et øyeblikk. *eht ury`•uh•blihk*	Hold on.
Jeg skal sette deg over. *yay skahl seht`•tuh day aw´•vuhr*	I'll put you through.
Han/Hun er ute for øyeblikket. *hahn/hewn ar ew´•tuh fohr ury`•uh•blihk•kuh*	He's/She's out at the moment.
Han/Hun kan ikke ta telefonen akkurat nå. *hahn/hewn kahn ihk`•kuh tah teh•luh•foon´•uhn ahk´•kew•raht naw*	He/She can't come to the phone right now.
Vil du legge igjen en beskjed? *vihl dew lehg`•guh ih•yehn´ ehn buh•sheh´*	Would you like to leave a message?
Ring igjen senere/om ti minutter. *rihng ih•yehn´ seh`•nuh•ruh/ohm tee mihn•ewt´•tuhr*	Call back later/in 10 minutes.
Kan han/hun ringe deg opp? *kahn hahn/hewn rihng`•uh day ohp*	Can he/she call you back?
Hva er nummeret ditt? *vah ar num´•muh•ruh diht*	What's your number?

Can I have your number?	**Kan jeg få nummeret ditt?** *kahn yay faw num´•muhr•uh diht*
My number is…	**Nummeret mitt er…** *num´•muhr•uh miht ar…*
Can you call me?	**Kan du ringe meg?** *kahn dew rihng`•uh may*
Can you text me?	**Kan du sende meg en tekstmelding?** *kahn dew sehn`•nuh may ehn tehkst´•mehl•lihng*
I'll call you.	**Jeg ringer deg.** *yay rihng`•uhr day*
I'll text you.	**Jeg sender deg en tekstmelding.** *yay sehn`•nuhr day ehn tehkst´•mehl•lihng*

Telephone Etiquette

Hello. This is…	**Hallo. Dette er…** *hah•loo´ deht`•tuh ar…*
Can I speak to…?	**Kan jeg få snakke med…?** *kahn yay faw snahk`•kuh meh…*
Extension…	**Linje…** *lihn`•yuh…*
Can you speak louder/ more slowly?	**Kan du snakke litt høyere/langsommere?** *kahn dew snahk`•kuh liht hury`•uhr•uh/lahng`•sohm•muhr•uh*
Can you repeat that?	**Kan du gjenta det?** *kahn dew yehn´•tah deh*
I'll call back later.	**Jeg ringer igjen senere.** *yay rihng`•uhr ih•yehn´ seh`•nuh•ruh*
Goodbye.	**Adjø.** *ahd•yur´*

Fax

Can I send/receive a fax here?	**Kan jeg sende/motta faks her?** *kahn yay sehn`•nu moot´•tah fahks har*
What's the fax number?	**Hva er faksnummeret?** *vah ar fahks´•num•muh•ru*
Please fax this to…	**Kan du fakse dette til…** *kahn dew fahks`•uh deht`•tuh tihl…*

Post

| Where's the post office/ mailbox [postbox]? | **Hvor finner jeg et postkontor/en postkasse?** *voo fihn´•nuhr yay eht pohst´•kun•toor/ehn pohst´•kahs•s* |

A stamp for this letter/ postcard, please.	**Et frimerke til dette brevet/kortet, takk.** *eht free´•mehrk•uh til <u>deht</u>`•tuh <u>breh</u>´•vuh/<u>kohr</u>´•tuh tahk*
How much?	**Hvor mye koster det?** *voor <u>mui</u>`•uh kohs`•tuhr deh*
I'd like to send this by airmail/express mail.	**Jeg vil gjerne sende dette med flypost/ekspress.** *yay vihl <u>ya</u>`r•nuh sehn`•nuh <u>deht</u>`•tuh meh flui•<u>pohst</u>/ ehks•<u>prehs</u>´*
Can I have a receipt?	**Kan jeg få kvittering?** *kahn yay faw kviht•<u>teh</u>´•rihng*

YOU MAY HEAR...

Kan du fylle ut en tolldeklarasjon? *kahn dew <u>fuil</u>`•luh ewt ehn <u>tohl</u>`•deh•klah•rah•shoon*	Can you fill out the customs declaration form?
Hva er verdien? *vah ar vehr•<u>dee</u>´•uhn*	What's the value?
Hva er det inni? *vah <u>ar</u> deh <u>ihn</u>`•ih*	What's inside?

Norwegian post offices are generally open Monday to Friday from 8:00 a.m. to 4:00 p.m. and Saturday from 9:00 a.m. to 1:00 p.m. Mailboxes are painted red and display the trumpet symbol of the post office.

Food & Drink

ESSENTIAL

Can you recommend a good restaurant/bar?	**Kan du anbefale en bra restaurant/bar?** *kahn dew* <u>*ahn*</u>`*-buh-**fah**-luh ehn br**ah** rehs-tew-<u>*rahng*</u>´*/b**ah**r*
Is there a traditional Norwegian/an inexpensive restaurant near here?	**Fins det en typisk norsk/billig restaurant i nærheten?** *fihns deh ehn* <u>*tui*</u>`*-pihsk nohrsk/*<u>*bihl*</u>`*-lih rehs-tew-*<u>*rahng*</u>´ *ih* <u>*nar*</u>´*-heh-tuhn*
A table for…	**Et bord til…** *eht boor tihl…*
Could we have a table here/there?	**Kan vi få et bord her/der?** *kahn vee faw eht eht boor har/dar*
Could we have a table in the corner?	**Kan vi få et hjørnebord?** *kahn vee faw eht eht* <u>*yur*</u>`*-uh-boor*
I'm waiting for someone.	**Jeg venter på noen.** *yay* <u>*vehn*</u>`*-tuhr poh* <u>*noo*</u>`*-uhn*
Where is the restroom [toilet]?	**Hvor er toalettet?** *voor ar tu-ah-*<u>*leht*</u>´*-tuh*
Can I have a menu?	**Kan jeg få se menyen?** *kahn yay faw seh meh-*<u>*nui*</u>´*-uhn*
What do you recommend?	**Hva kan du anbefale?** *vah kahn dew* <u>*ahn*</u>´*-buh-**fah**-luh*
I'd like…	**Jeg vil gjerne ha…** *yay vihl* <u>*ya*</u>`*r-nuh hah…*
Can I have more…?	**Kan jeg få litt mer…?** *kahn yay faw liht mehr…*
Enjoy your meal!	**God appetitt!** *gu ahp-puh-*<u>*tiht*</u>´
Can I have the check [bill]?	**Kan jeg få regningen?** *kahn yay faw* <u>*ray*</u>`*-nihng-uhn*
Is service included?	**Er service inkludert?** *ar* <u>*surr*</u>´*-vihs ing-klew-*<u>*dehrt*</u>´
Can I pay by credit card?	**Kan jeg betale med kredittkort?** *kahn yay buh-*<u>*tah*</u>´*-luh meh kreh-*<u>*diht*</u>´*-kohrt*

| Can I have a receipt? | **Kan jeg få kvittering?** *kahn yay faw* kviht‑*teh*´‑rihng |
| Thank you. | **Takk.** *tahk* |

Where to Eat

Can you recommend...?	**Kan du anbefale...?** *kahn dew ahn*´‑buh‑*fah*‑luh...
a restaurant	**en restaurant** *ehn rehs‑tew‑rahng*´
a bar	**en bar** *ehn bahr*
a cafe	**en kafé** *ehn kah‑feh*´
an authentic/a non-touristy restaurant	**en autentisk/turistfri restaurant** *ehn ev‑tehn‑tihsk/tew‑rihst‑free rehs‑tew‑rahng*
a cheap restaurant	**en billig restaurant** *ehn bihl‑ih rehs‑tew‑rahng*
an expensive restaurant	**en dyr restaurant** *ehn dyr rehs‑tew‑rahng*
a fast-food place	**en hurtigmatrestaurant** *ehn hewr*`‑*tih‑maht‑rehs‑tew‑rahng*
a restaurant with a good view	**en restaurant med god utsikt** *ehn rehs‑tew‑rahng meh gu ewt‑sihkt*

Reservations & Preferences

I'd like to reserve a table...	**Jeg vil gjerne bestille et bord...** *yay vihl ya*`*r‑nuh buhs‑tihl*´*‑luh eht boor...*
for four	**til fire** *tihl fee*`‑*ruh*
for this evening	**til i kveld** *tihl ih kvehl*
for tomorrow at...	**til i morgen klokken...** *tihl ih maw*`‑*ruhn klohk*`‑*kuhn...*
A table for two, please.	**Et bord til to, takk.** *eht boor*´ *tihl too tahk*
We have a reservation.	**Vi har bestilt bord.** *vee hahr buhs‑tihlt*´ *boor*
My name is...	**Jeg heter...** *yay heh*`‑*tuhr...*

YOU MAY SEE...

INNGANGSPENGER	cover charge
DAGENS MENY	menu of the day
SPESIALITETER	specials
TIPS (IKKE) INKLUDERT	service (not) included

Could we have...?	**Kan vi få et...?**	_kahn vee faw..._
a table here/there	**et bord her/der**	_eht boor har/dar_
a table in the corner	**et hjørnebord**	_eht <u>yur`</u>•nuh•boor_
a table by the window	**vindusbord**	_<u>vihn`</u>•dews•boor_
Can we sit...	**Kan vi sitte...**	_kahn vee siht•eh_
outside	**ute**	_ewte_
in the shade	**i skyggen**	_ee shyh•gehn_
in the sun	**i solen**	_ee sul•ehn_
in a non-smoking area	**i et røykfritt område**	_ee eht ruryk•friht um•raw•deh_
Where is the restroom [toilet]?	**Hvor er toalettet?**	_voor ar tu•ah•<u>leht´</u>•tuh_

For Time, see page 171.

How to Order

Waiter/Waitress!	**Servitør!** *ser•vih•turr´*	
We're ready to order.	**Vi er klare til å bestille.** *vee ar <u>klah</u>`•ruh tihl aw buhs•<u>tihl</u>´•luh*	
Can I have the wine list?	**Kan jeg få se vinkartet?** *kahn yay faw seh <u>veen</u>`•kahr•tuh*	
I'd like…	**Jeg vil gjerne ha…** *yay vihl <u>ya</u>`r•nuh hah…*	
a bottle of…	**en flaske…** *ehn <u>flahs</u>`•kuh…*	
a carafe of…	**en karaffel…** *ehn kah•<u>rahf</u>´•fuhl…*	
a glass of…	**et glass…** *eht glahs…*	
Can I have a menu?	**Kan jeg få se menyen?** *kahn yay faw seh meh•<u>nui</u>´•uhn*	

YOU MAY HEAR…

Har dere bestilt bord? *hahr <u>deh</u>•ruh buhs•<u>tihlt</u>´ boor*	Do you have a reservation?
Hvor mange? *voor mahn•geh*	How many?
Røyk eller røykfritt? *ruryk ehl•ehr ruryk•friht*	Smoking or non-smoking?
Er dere klare til å bestille? *ar deh•ruh <u>klah</u>´•ruh tihl aw buhs•<u>tihl</u>´•luh*	Are you ready to order?
Hva skal det være? *vah skahl deh <u>va</u>`•ruh*	What would you like?
Jeg anbefaler… *yay ahn•beh•fahl•ehr*	I recommend…
God appetitt. *gu ahp•puh•<u>tiht</u>´*	Enjoy your meal.

Do you have…?	**Har dere…?**	*hahr deh`•ruh…*
a menu in English	**en meny på engelsk**	*ehn meh•nui´ poh ehng´•ehlsk*
a set menu	**en fast meny**	*ehn fahst meh•nui´*
a children's menu	**en barnemeny**	*ehn bahr`•nuh•meh•nui*
What do you recommend?	**Hva kan du anbefale?**	*vah kahn dew ahn´•buh•fah•luh*
What's this?	**Hva er dette?**	*vah ar deht`•tuh*
What's in it?	**Hva inneholder den/det?**	*vah ihn`•nuh•hawl•luhr dehn/deh*
Is it spicy?	**Er den/det sterkt krydret?**	*ar dehn/deh sterkt kruid`•ruht*
rare	**råstekt**	*raw`•stehkt*
medium	**medium stekt**	*meh´•dih•ewm stehkt*
well-done	**godt stekt**	*goht stehkt*
Can I have more…?	**Kan jeg få litt mer…?**	*kahn yay faw liht mehr…*
With/Without…	**Med/Uten…**	*meh/ew`•tuhn…*
I can't eat…	**Jeg tåler ikke…**	*yay taw´•luhr ihk`•kuh…*
It's to go [take away].	**Jeg tar det med meg.**	*yay tahr´ deh meh may*

For Grammar, see page 165.

Cooking Methods

baked	**bakt**	bahkt
boiled	**kokt**	kukt
braised	**braisert**	brahs·_seh_´rt
breaded	**panert**	pah·_neh_´rt
creamed	**fløtegratinert**	_flur_´·tuh·grah·tih·nehrt
diced	**i terninger**	ih _ter_`·nihng·uhr
fried	**stekt**	stehkt
grilled (broiled)	**grillet**	_grihl_`·luht
poached	**pochert**	pu·_sheh_´rt
roasted	**ovnsstekt**	_ohvns_`·stehkt
sautéed	**sautert**	soh·_teh_´rt
smoked	**røkt**	rurkt
steamed	**dampet**	_dahm_`·puht
stewed	**stuet**	_stew_`·uht
stuffed	**fylt**	fuilt

62

Dietary Requirements

I'm…	**Jeg er…**	yay ar…
a diabetic	**diabetiker**	dih·ah·_beh_´·tihk·uhr
lactose intolerant	**laktoseintolerant**	lahk·_too_`·suh·ihn·toh·luh·rahnt
a vegetarian	**vegetarianer**	veh·guh·tahr·ih·_ah_´·nuhr
vegan	**veganer**	veh·gah·nehr
I'm allergic to…	**Jeg er allergisk mot…**	yay ar ah·_lehr_´·gihsk moot…
I can't eat…	**Jeg kan ikke spise…**	yay kahn _ihk_`·kuh _spee_`·suh.
dairy	**melkeprodukter**	_mehl_`·kuh·pru·dewk·tuhr
gluten	**gluten**	_glew_´·tuhn
nuts	**nøtter**	_nurt_´·tuhr
pork	**svinekjøtt**	_svee_`·nuh·khurt
shellfish	**skalldyr**	_skahl_`·duir
spicy foods	**sterkt krydret mat**	sterkt _kruid_`·ruht m**ah**t
wheat	**hvete**	_veh_`·tuh

s it halal/kosher?	**Er maten halal/kosher?** *ar <u>mah</u> ´t•uhn hahl•<u>ahl</u> ´/ <u>kohsh</u> ´•uhr*
Do you have...?	**Har dere?** *hahr dehr•eh*
skimmed milk	**skummet melk** *sku•meht mehlk*
whole milk	**helmelk** *hehl•mehlk*
soya milk	**soyamelk** *soy•ah•mehlk*

Dining with Children

Do you have children's portions?	**Har dere barneporsjoner?** *hahr deh`•ruh <u>bahr</u>`•nuh•poor•sh<u>oo</u>n•uhr*
Can I have a highchair/child's seat?	**Kan jeg få en babystol/barnestol?** *kahn yay faw ehn <u>beh</u>`•bih•stool/<u>bahr</u>`•nuh•stool*
Where can I feed/ change the baby?	**Hvor kan jeg amme/bytte på babyen?** *voor kahn yay <u>ah</u>`•muh/<u>buit</u>`•tuh poh <u>beh</u>´•bih•uhn*
Can you warm this?	**Kan du varme opp denne?** *kahn dew <u>vahr</u>`•muh ohp <u>dehn</u>`•nuh*

How to Complain

How much longer will our food be?	**Hvor lenge drøyer det med maten?** *vur <u>lehng</u>`•uh <u>drury</u>`•uhr deh meh <u>maht</u>´•uhn*
We can't wait any longer.	**Vi kan ikke vente lenger.** *vee kahn <u>ihk</u>`•kuh <u>vehn</u>`•tuh <u>lehng</u>`•uhr*
We're leaving.	**Vi drar.** *vee drahr*
That's not what I ordered.	**Dette er ikke det jeg bestilte.** <u>deht</u>`•tuh ar <u>ihk</u>`•kuh deh yay buh•<u>stihl</u>`•tuh*
I asked for...	**Jeg ba om...** *yay bah um...*
I can't eat this.	**Jeg kan ikke spise dette.** *yay kahn <u>ihk</u>`•kuh <u>spee</u>`•suh <u>deht</u>`•tuh*

This is too...	**Det er for...** *deh ar fohr...*
cold/hot	**kaldt/varmt** *kahlt/varmt*
salty/spicy	**salt/krydret** *sahlt/kruid`·ruht*
tough/bland	**seigt/mildt** *saykt/mihlt*
This isn't clean/fresh.	**Dette er ikke rent/ferskt.** *deht`·tuh ar ihk`·kuh rehnt/ferskt*

Paying

Can I have the check [bill]?	**Kan jeg får regningen?** *kahn yay faw rayn`·nihng·uhn*
We'd like to pay separately.	**Vi vil gjerne betale hver for oss.** *vee vihl yar`·nuh buh·tah´·luh var fohr ohs*
It's all together.	**Det er for alt sammen.** *deh ar fohr ahlt sam·muhn*
Is service included?	**Er service inkludert?** *ar surr´·vihs ihng·klew·dehrt´*
What's this amout for?	**Hva står dette beløpet for?** *vah stawr deht`·tuh buh·lur´·puh fohr*
I didn't have that. I had...	**Jeg spiste ikke det. Jeg spiste...** *yay spihs`·tuh ihk`·kuh deh yay spihs`·tuh...*
Can I pay by credit card?	**Kan jeg betale med kredittkort?** *kahn yay buh·tah´·luh meh kreh·diht´·kort*
Can I have an itemized bill/a receipt?	**Kan jeg få en spesifisert regning/en kvittering?** *kahn yay faw ehn speh·sih·fih·seh´rt ray`·nihng/ehn kviht·teh´·rihng*
That was a very good meal.	**Maten smakte veldig godt.** *maht´·uhn smahk`·tuh vehl´·dih goht*
I've already paid.	**Jeg har allerede betalt.** *yay hahr ahl·eh·rehd·eh beh·tahlt*

A 10-15% service charge is typically included in most restaurant bills, though wait staff often receive an extra 5-10% tip.

Meals & Cooking

Breakfast

appelsinjuice *ahp• puhl•<u>see</u>´n•yews*	orange juice
appelsinmarmelade *ahp•puhl•<u>see</u>´n•mahr•muh•<u>lah</u>•duh*	orange marmalade
brød *brur*	bread
bløtkokt/hardkokt egg <u>*blur*</u>`*t•kukt/* <u>*hah*</u>`*r•kukt ehg*	soft-boiled/hard-boiled eggs
egg og bacon/skinke *ehg aw <u>bay</u>´•kuhn/ <u>hihng</u>`•kuh*	eggs with bacon/ham
eggerøre <u>*ehg*</u>´•*guh•<u>rur</u>•ruh*	scrambled eggs
frokostblanding <u>*froo*</u>´•*kohst•blahn•nihng*	cereal
grapefruktjuice <u>*grehp*</u>´•*frewkt•yews*	grapefruit juice
havregrøt <u>*hahv*</u>`•*ruh•grurt*	oatmeal [porridge]
honning <u>*hohn*</u>`•*nihng*	honey
juice *yews*	fruit juice
svart/koffeinfri kaffe *svahrt/ <u>kohf</u>•fuh•<u>ee</u>´n• free <u>kahf</u>´•fuh*	black/decaffeinated coffee
kaffe med melk/fløte <u>*kahf*</u>´•*fuh meh mehlk/<u>flur</u>`•tuh*	coffee with milk/cream
omelett *oh•muh•<u>leht</u>´*	omelet
ost *ust*	cheese
ristet brød <u>*rihs*</u>`•*tuht brur*	toast
rundstykke <u>*rewn*</u>´•*stuik•kuh*	roll
smør *smurr*	butter
speilegg <u>*spayl*</u>´•*ehg*	fried egg
syltetøy <u>*suil*</u>´•*tuh•tury*	jam
te med melk/sitron *teh meh mehlk/ siht•<u>roo</u>´n*	tea with milk/lemon
varm sjokolade *vahrm shu•ku•<u>lah</u>`•duh*	hot chocolate

varmt vann *varmt vahn*	hot water
yoghurt <u>*yoo*</u>´·*gewrt*	yogurt

> **Frokost** (breakfast) is usually eaten early and consists of coffee
> or tea and **smørbrød** (open-faced sandwiches) and perhaps
> cereal. **Lunsj** (lunch) is typically a light meal and may consist of
> a simple **matpakke** (open-faced sandwich brought from home).
> **Middag** (dinner) is often the only hot meal of the day. If **middag** is
> eaten early, then **aftens** (a late night snack), consisting of bread or
> crackers with butter or cheese and cold cuts, is eaten to get through the
> night without going hungry.

Appetizers

blåskjell <u>*blaw*</u>`·*shehl*	mussels
fenalår <u>*feh*</u>`·*nah·lawr*	cured leg of mutton
ferske reker <u>*fehrs*</u>`·*kuh* <u>*reh*</u>`·*kuhr*	unshelled shrimp [prawns]
fiskekabaret <u>*fihs*</u>`·*kuh·kah·bah·r*e**h**	assorted seafood and vegetables in aspic
gåselever <u>*gaw*</u>`·*suh·leh·vuhr*	goose liver

gravlaks _grahv_`·lahks	cured salmon flavored with dill
hummer _hum_´·muhr	lobster
kamskjell _kahm_`·shehl	scallop
kaviar kah·vih·**ah**´r	caviar
krabbe _krahb_`·buh	crab
laks lahks	salmon
rakørret _rahk_`·urr·ruht	specially processed, salt-cured and fermented trout
rekecocktail _reh_`·kuh·kohk·tayl	shrimp [prawn] cocktail
røkelaks _rur_`·kuh·lahks	smoked salmon
sildebrikke _sihl_`·luh·brihk·kuh	a variety of herring, served with bread and butter
skinke _shihng_`·kuh	ham
spekepølse _speh_`·kuh·purl·suh	smoked, cured sausage
spekeskinke _speh_`·kuh·shihng·kuh	smoked, cured ham
sursild _sewr_´sihl	marinated herring
østers _urs_´·tehrs	oysters

Soup

aspargessuppe ahs·_pahr_´·guhs·sewp·puh	asparagus soup
betasuppe _beh_`·tah·sewp·puh	thick meat and vegetable soup
blomkålsuppe _blohm_´·kawl·sewp·puh	cauliflower soup
buljong bewl·_yohng_´	consommé
fiskesuppe _fihs_`·kuh·sewp·puh	fish soup
fransk løksuppe frahnsk _lur_`k·sewp·puh	French onion soup
grønnsaksuppe _grurn_`·sahk·sewp·puh	vegetable soup
gul ertesuppe gewl _er_`·tuh·sewp·puh	yellow pea soup
hummersuppe _hum_`·muhr·sewp·puh	lobster soup
kjøttsuppe _khurt_`·sewp·puh	meat soup

løksuppe _lur`k·sewp·puh_	onion soup
neslesuppe _nehs`·luh·sewp·puh_	nettle soup
oksehalesuppe _ohk`·suh·hah·luh·sewp·puh_	oxtail soup
sellerisuppe _seh·luh·ree´·sewp·puh_	celery soup
sjampinjongsuppe	button mushroom soup
shahm·pihn·yohng´·sewp·puh	
soppsuppe _sohp`·sewp·puh_	field mushroom soup
tomatsuppe _tu·mah´t·sewp·puh_	tomato soup

> Norwegian cuisine features a wide range of soups, which are
> often eaten with **flatbrød** (a thin, barley and wheat or barley
> and rye cracker); this is a common starter. **Fiskesuppe** (fish soup)
> is very popular along the coast. Other traditional soups involve meat,
> such as **betasuppe** (meat and vegetable soup), or vegetables, like **gul
> ertesuppe** (yellow pea soup).

Fish & Seafood

abbor _ahb`·bohr_	perch
akkar _ahk`·kahr_	squid
ansjos _ahn·shoo´s_	anchovies or marinated sprats
blåskjell _blaw`·shehl_	mussels
blekksprut _blehk`·sprewt_	octopus
brasme _brahs`·muh_	bream
breiflabb _bray`·flahb_	angler, also called frogfish o goosefish
dampet ørret _dahm`·puht urr`·ruht_	poached trout
fisk _fihsk_	fish
fiskeboller _fihs`·kuh·bohl·luhr_	fish balls

fiskekaker _fihs`·kuh·**kah**·kuhr_ — fried fish cakes

fiskepudding _fihs`·kuh·pewd·dihng_ — fish pudding

flyndre _fluin`·druh_ — flounder

fritert flyndrefilet _friht·**eh**`rt fluin`·druh·fih·**leh**_ — deep fried flounder fillet

gjedde _yehd`·duh_ — pike

gravlaks _grah`v·lahks_ — cured salmon flavored with dill

hellefisk _hehl`·luh·fihsk_ — halibut

hummer _hum`·muhr_ — lobster

hvitting _viht`·tihng_ — whiting

hyse _hui`·suh_ — haddock (western Norway)

kamskjell _kahm`·shel_ — scallop

karpe _kahr`·puh_ — carp

klippfisk _klihp`·fihsk_ — salted and dried fish

kokt torsk _kukt tohrsk_ — poached cod

kokt ørret _kukt urr`·ruht_ — poached trout

kolje _kohl`·yuh_ — haddock (eastern Norway)

krabbe _krahb`·buh_ — crab

kreps _krehps_ — freshwater crayfish

kveite _kvay`·tuh_ — halibut

laks _lahks_ — salmon

lutefisk _lew`_•tuh•fihsk	stockfish soaked in lye
lysing _lui`_•sihng	hake
makrell mahk•_rehl´_	mackerel
piggvar _pihg`_•vahr	turbot
plukkfisk _pluk´_•fihsk	stewed codfish
regnbueørret _rayn`_•bew•uh•urr•ruht	rainbow trout
reker _reh`_•kuhr	shrimp [prawns]
rogn rohngn	roe
rødspette _rur`_•speht•tuh	plaice
sardell sar•_dehl´_	canned anchovy
sardin sar•_dee´n_	sardine
sei say	pollock
sik seek	whitefish
sild sihl	herring
sjømat _shur`_•maht	seafood
sjøørret _shur`_•urr•ruht	sea trout
sjøtunge _shur`_•tung•uh	sole
skalldyr _skahl´_•duir	shellfish
spekesild _speh`_•kuh•sihl	salted herring
steinbit _stayn`_•beet	catfish
stør sturr	sturgeon
størje _sturr`_•yuh	tuna
torsk tohrsk	cod
tunfisk _tew`n_•fihsk	tuna
tørrfisk _turr´_•fihsk	stockfish
uer _ew`_•uhr	rosefish
ørret _urr`_•ruht	trout
østers _urs´_•tehrs	oysters
åbor _aw`_•bohr	perch
ål awl	eel

Meat & Poultry

and *ahn* — duck

bacon *bay´-kuhn* — bacon

benløse fugler *beh`n-lurs-uh few`l-uhr* — fried, rolled and stuffed slices of veal or beef

biff *bihf* — beef steak

biff med løk *bihf meh lurk* — thick beef steak topped with fried onion

broiler *broi´-luhr* — chicken

brun lapskaus *brewn lahps´-kevs* — Norwegian stew in brown gravy

dyrestek *dui`-ruh-stehk* — roast venison

elg *ehlg* — moose

elgbiff *ehlg`-bihf* — moose steak

elgfilet *ehlg`-fih-leh* — moose fillet

elgstek *ehlg`-stehk* — roast moose

fårestek *faw`-ruh-stehk* — roast leg of mutton or lamb

fårekjøtt *faw´-ruh-khurt* — mutton

fårikål *faw´-rih-kawl* — mutton or lamb in cabbage stew

fasan *fah-sah´n* — pheasant

gås *gaws* — goose

hare *hah`-ruh* — hare

hjort *yohrt* — deer

høne *hur`-nuh* — hen

hvalbiff *vahl`-bihf* — whale steak

kalkun *kahl-kew´n* — turkey

kalvebrissel *kahl`-vuh-brihs-suhl* — calf's sweetbread

kalvekjøtt *kahl`-vuh-khurt* — veal

kalvelever *kahl`-vuh-lehv-vuhr* — calf's liver

kanin *kah-nee´n* — rabbit

karbonade *kahr·bu·nah`·duh*		hamburger
kjøttboller *khurt*		meatballs
kjøttkaker *khurt`·kahk·uhr*		small hamburgers
kjøttpudding *khurt`·pud·dihng*		meatloaf
knoke *knoo`·kuh*		bone
kotelett *koh·tuh·leht´*		chop
kylling *khuil`·lihng*		chicken
lammekjøtt *lahm`·muh·khurt*		lamb
lapskaus *lahps´·kehvs*		Norwegian stew with meat, potatoes and root vegetable
lever *lehv´·vuhr*		liver
lys lapskaus *luis lahps´·kehvs*		Norwegian stew with diced, salted boiled pork
medisterkaker *meh·dihs´·tuhr·kah·kuhr*		small pork and beef hamburgers
medisterpølse *meh·dihs´·tuhr·purl·suh*		pork and beef sausage
mørbradstek *mur`·r·brahd·stehk*		roast sirloin
nyrer *nui`·ruhr*		kidneys
oksebryst *ohk`·suh·bruist*		beef brisket
oksekjøtt *ohk`·suh·khurt*		beef
okserulader *ohk`·suh·rewl·lah·duhr*		braised beef rolls
oksestek *ohk`·suh·stehk*		roast beef
orrfugl *ohr`·fewl*		black grouse, a woodland bird
pinnekjøtt *pihn`·nuh·khurt*		salted and dried mutton ribs steamed on twigs
pytt i panne *puit·ih·pah`·nuh*		hash or meat and vegetable
pølse *purl`·suh*		sausage
rådyr *raw´·duir*		roe-deer
rapphøne *rahp`·hur·nuh*		partridge
reinsdyr *rayns´·duir*		reindeer

ribbe <u>rihb</u>`·buh	spareribs
rype <u>rui</u>`·puh	grouse, a mountain bird
skinke <u>shihng</u>`·kuh	ham
spekeskinke <u>speh</u>`·kuh·shihng·kuh	smoked, cured ham
stek stehk	roast (beef, reindeer, moose, etc.)
svinekjøtt <u>svee</u>`·nuh·khurt	pork
svor svoor	bacon rind [crackling]
sylte <u>suil</u>`·tuh	head cheese [brawn]
tartarbiff tahr·<u>tah</u>´r·bihf	steak tartare
T-benstek <u>teh</u>´·behn·stehk	T-bone steak
vaktel <u>vahk</u>´·tuhl	quail
villand <u>vihl</u>`·lahn	wild duck
wienerschnitzel <u>vee</u>`·nuhr·shniht·suhl	breaded veal cutlet

Vegetables & Staples

agurk ah·<u>gewr</u>´k	cucumber
anisfrø <u>ah</u>`·nihs·frur	aniseed
artisjokker ar·tih·<u>shohk</u>`·kuhr	artichokes
asparges ahs·<u>pahr</u>´·guhs	asparagus
aubergine aw·buhr·<u>shee</u>´n	eggplant [aubergine]
basilikum bah·<u>see</u>´·lih·kewm	basil
blomkål <u>blohm</u>´·kawl	cauliflower
bønner <u>burn</u>`·nuhr	beans
brokkoli <u>brohk</u>´·koh·lih	broccoli
dill dihl	dill
erter <u>ehr</u>´·tuhr	peas
gresskar <u>grehs</u>`·kahr	pumpkin
gressløk <u>grehs</u>`·lurk	chives
grønnkål <u>grurn</u>´·kawl	kale

gulrøtter _gew`l•rurt•tuhr_	carrots
hodesalat _hoo`•duh•sah•laht_	lettuce
hvitløk _vee`t•lurk_	garlic
ingefær _ihng´•uh•far_	ginger
kål _kawl_	cabbage
kanel _kah•neh`l_	cinnamon
kantareller _kahn•tah•rehl´•luhr_	chanterelle mushrooms
kapers _kah`•puhrs_	capers
karri _kahr´•rih_	curry seasoning
karve _kahr`•vuh_	caraway seeds
kokte poteter _kuk`•tuh pu•teh`t•uhr_	boiled potatoes
komler/komper _kum`•luhr/kum`•puhr_	potato dumplings
linser _lihn`•suhr_	lentils
løk _lurk_	onions
mais _mies_	corn
maiskolbe _mies´•kohl•buh_	corn on the cob
nellik _nehl´•lihk_	clove
nepe _neh`•puh_	turnip
nudler _newd´•luhr_	noodles
nypoteter _nui`•pu•teht•uhr_	new potatoes
paprika _pahp´•rih•kah_	sweet pepper
persille _pehr•sihl´•luh_	parsley

ommes frites *pohm friht*	French fries [chips]
otet *pu·teh´t*	potato
otetgull *pu·teh´t·gewl*	potato chips [crisps]
otetkroketter *pu·teh´t·krohk·keht·tuhr*	potato croquettes
otetmos *pu·teh´t·moos*	mashed potatoes
otetsalat *pu·teh´t·sah·laht*	potato salad
urre *pewr`·ruh*	leeks
aspeball *rahs`·puh·bahl*	potato dumplings
eddiker *rehd´·dihk·kuhr*	radishes
is *rees*	rice
osenkål *roo´·suhn·kawl*	Brussels sprouts
ødbeter *rur´·beh·tuhr*	beet [beetroot]
ødkål *rur´·kawl*	red cabbage
alat *sah·lah´t*	salad
alvie *sahl·vee`·uh*	sage
elleri *sehl·luhr·ee´*	celery
ildeball *sihl´·luh·bahl*	potato dumplings filled with minced salted herring
tekte poteter *stehk`·tuh pu·teh´t·uhr*	sautéed potatoes
tuede poteter *stew`·eh·duh pu·teh´t·uhr*	potatoes in a white sauce
jampinjonger *sham·pihn·yohng´·uhr*	button mushrooms
opp *sohp*	mushrooms
pinat *spih·nah´t*	spinach
urkål *sew´r·kawl*	coleslaw
ylteagurk *suil`·tuh·ah·gewrk*	pickle
imian *tee´·mih·ahn*	thyme
omater *tu·maht´·uhr*	tomatoes

Fruit

ananas *ahn´·nah·nahs*	pineapple
appelsin *ahp·puhl·see´n*	orange
aprikos *ahp·rih·koo´s*	apricot

banan _bah·<u>nah</u>´n_	banana
bjørnebær <u>byur</u>`·nuh·bar_	blackberries
blåbær <u>blaw</u>`·bar_	blueberries
bringebær <u>brihng</u>´·uh·bar_	raspberries
dadler <u>dahd</u>´·luhr_	dates
druer <u>drew</u>`·uhr_	grapes
einebær _ay_`·nuh·bar_	juniper berries
eple <u>ehp</u>`·luh_	apple
fersken <u>fehrs</u>´·kuhn_	peach
fikener <u>fee</u>´·kuhn·uhr_	figs
grapefrukt <u>grehp</u>´·frewkt_	grapefruit
hasselnøtter <u>hahs</u>´·suhl·nurt·tuhr_	hazelnuts
jordbær <u>yoo</u>´r·bar_	strawberries
kastanjer _kahs·<u>tahn</u>´·yuhr_	chestnuts
kirsebær <u>khihr</u>´·suh·bar_	cherries
kokosnøtt <u>kuk</u>´·kus·nurt_	coconut
korinter _ku·<u>rihn</u>´·tuhr_	currants
mandarin _mahn·dah·<u>ree</u>´n_	tangerine
mandler <u>mahn</u>´d·luhr_	almonds
markjordbær <u>mahr</u>`k·yoor·bar_	wild strawberries
melon _meh·<u>loo</u>´n_	melon

molter/multer _mohl`-tuhr/mewl`-tuhr_ — arctic cloudberries

moreller _mu-rehl´-luhr_ — morello cherries

nektarin _nehk-tah-ree´n_ — nectarine

nøtter _nurt´-tuhr_ — nuts

peanøtter _pee´-ah-nurt-tuhr_ — peanuts

plommer _plum`-muhr_ — plums

pære _pa`-ruh_ — pear

rabarbra _rah-bahr´-brah_ — rhubarb

rips _rihps_ — red currants

rognebær _rohng`-nuh-bar_ — rowanberries

rosiner _ru-see´-nuhr_ — raisins

sitron _siht-roo´n_ — lemon

solbær _soo`l-bar_ — black currants

stikkelsbær _stihk`-kuhls-bar_ — gooseberries

svisker _svihs`-kuhr_ — prunes

tranebær _trah`-nuh-bar_ — cranberries

tyttebær _tuit´-tuh-bar_ — lingonberry

valnøtter _vahl`-nurt-tuhr_ — walnuts

vannmelon _vahn`-meh-loon_ — watermelon

Cheese

ekte geitost _ehk`-tuh yayt`-ust_ — goat cheese

fløtemysost _flur`-tuh-muis-ust_ — mild and sweet cow's milk cheese

gammelost _gahm`-muhl-ust_ — pungent cheese made with skimmed milk

gudbrandsdalsost _gewd`-brahns-dahls-ust_ — cow and goat's milk cheese

jarlsbergost _yahrls´-behrg-ust_ — mild, slightly sweet, semi-hard cheese

normannaost _noor-mahn´-nah-ust_ — blue-veined cow's milk cheese

ridderost _rihd´-duhr-ust_ — semi-hard cheese with nutty flavor

Dessert

bløtkake _blur`t·kah·kuh_ — layer cake

fruktkompott _frewkt´·kohm·poht_ — stewed fruit

hoffdessert _hohf´·dehs·sar_ — layers of meringue and whipped cream, topped with chocolate sauce and toasted almonds

is _ees_ — ice cream

karamellpudding _kah·rah·mehl´·pewd·dihng_ — creme caramel

krem _krehm_ — whipped cream

mandelkake _mahn´·duhl·kah·kuh_ — almond cake

molter/multer med krem _mohl´·tuhr/mewl`tuhr meh krehm_ — arctic cloudberries with whipped cream

pære Belle Helene _pa`·ruh behl heh·leh´n_ — poached pears with vanilla ice cream and chocolate

pannekaker _pahn`·nuh·kah·kuhr_ — pancakes

riskrem _ree´s·krehm_ — creamed rice

rødgrøt med fløte _rur`·grurt meh flur`·tuh_ — berry compote with cream

sjokoladepudding _shu·ku·lah`·duh·pewd·dihng_ — chocolate pudding

sorbett _sohr·beht´_ — sorbet

sufflé _sewf·leh´_ — soufflé

terte _tehr`·tuh_ — fruit cake

tilslørte bondepiker _tihl´·slurr·tuh bun´·nuh·pee·kuhr_ — layers of stewed apples, cookie [biscuit] crumbs, and whipped cream

vafler med syltetøy _vahf´·luhr meh suil`·tuh·tury_ — waffles with jam

vaniljesaus _vah·nihl´·yuh·sevs_ — vanilla sauce

varm eplekake med krem _vahrm ehp`·luh·kah·kuh meh krehm_ — hot apple pie with whipped cream

Sauces & Condiments

ketchup	**ketchup** kat·shewp
mustard	**sennep** sehn·ehp
pepper	**pepper** _pehp´·puhr_
salt	**salt** sahlt

At the Market

Where are the carts [trolleys]/baskets?	**Hvor er handlevognene/handlekurvene?** voor **a**r _hahn`d·luh_·vohng·nuh·nuh/ _hahn`d·luh·kewr·vuh·nuh_
Where is…?	**Hvor er…?** voor **a**r…
Can I have some of that/those?	**Kan jeg få litt av det/dem?** kahn yay f**aw** liht a deh/dehm
Can I taste it?	**Kan jeg smake?** kahn yay _sm**ah**`·kuh_

In Norway, there are a few large supermarket chains, such as Rimi, Rema and Kiwi, in addition to many local mini-markets. Keep in mind that supermarkets do not accept credit cards, so remember to bring cash when you go shopping for groceries.

Measurements in Europe are metric - and that applies to the weight of food too. If you tend to think in pounds and ounces, it's worth brushing up on what the metric equivalent is before you go shopping for fruit and veg in markets and supermarkets. Five hundred grams, or half a kilo, is a common quantity to order, and that converts to just over a pound (17.65 ounces, to be precise).

I'd like...	**Jeg vil gjerne ha...** *yay vihl yar`•nuh hah...*
a (half) kilo of...	**en (halv) kilo...** *ehn (hahl) khee´•lu...*
a (half) liter of...	**en (halv) liter...** *ehn (hahl) lee´•tuhr...*
a piece of...	**et stykke...** *eht stuik`•kuh...*
a slice of...	**en skive...** *ehn shee`•vuh...*
More/Less than that.	**Mer/Mindre enn det.** *mehr/mihn´•druh ehn deh*
How much?	**Hvor mye koster det?** *voor mew`•uh kohs`•tuhr deh*
Where do I pay?	**Hvor betaler man?** *voor buh•tah´•luhr mahn*
Can I have a bag?	**Kan jeg få en bærepose?** *kahn yay faw ehn ba`•ruh•poo•suh*
I'm being helped.	**Jeg blir ekspedert.** *yay bleer ehks•puh•deh´rt*

For Conversion Tables, see page 175.

YOU MAY HEAR...

Kan jeg hjelpe deg? *kahn yay yehl`•puh day*	Can I help you?
Hva skal det være? *vah skahl deh va`•ruh*	What would you like?
Skal det være noe annet? *skahl deh va`•ruh noo`•uh ahn`•nuht*	Anything else?
Det blir...kroner, takk. *deh bleer... kroo`n•uhr tahk*	That's...kroner, please.

In the Kitchen

bottle opener	**en flaskeåpner** *ehn <u>flahs</u>`·kuh·**awp**·nuhr*
bowls	**skåler** *<u>skaw</u>`·luhr*
can opener	**en boksåpner** *ehn <u>bohks</u>`·**awp**·nuhr*
cheese slicer	**ostehøvel** *<u>us</u>`·tuh·hur·vuhl*
corkscrew	**en korketrekker** *ehn <u>kohr</u>`·kuh·trehk·kuhr*
cups	**kopper** *<u>kohp</u>`·puhr*
forks	**gafler** *<u>gahf</u>´·luhr*
frying pan	**en stekepanne** *ehn <u>steh</u>`·kuh·pahn·nuh*
glasses	**glass** *glahs*
knives	**kniver** *<u>kneev</u>`·uhr*
measuring cup/	**et målebeger/en måleskje** *eht <u>maw</u>`·luh·beh·guhr/*
measuring spoon	*ehn <u>maw</u>`·luh·sheh*
napkins	**papirservietter** *pah·<u>pee</u>´r·serv·yeht·tuhr*
plates	**tallerkener** *tah·<u>lehr</u>´·kuhn·uhr*
pot	**en gryte** *ehn <u>grui</u>`·tuh*
saucepan	**en kasserolle** *ehn kah·suh·<u>rohl</u>`·luh*
spatula	**en slikkepott** *ehn <u>slihk</u>`·kuh·poht*
spoons	**skjeer** *sheh`·uhrv*

Drinks

ESSENTIAL

Can I have the wine list/drink menu?	**Kan jeg få se vinkartet/drikkekartet?** *kahn yay faw seh veen`·kahr·tuh/drihk`·kuh·kahr·tuh*
What do you recommend?	**Hva kan du anbefale?** *vah kahn dew ahn´·buh·fah·luh*
Can I have the house wine?	**Kan jeg få husets vin?** *kahn yay faw hew´s·uhs veen*
Can I buy you a drink?	**Kan jeg by på en drink?** *kahn yay bui poh ehn drihng*
Cheers!	**Skål!** *skawl*
A coffee/tea, please.	**En kaffe/te, takk.** *ehn kahf´·fuh/teh tahk*
Black.	**Svart.** *svahrt*
With…	**Med…** *meh…*
milk	**melk** *mehlk*
sugar	**sukker** *suk`·kuhr*
artificial sweetener	**søtningsmiddel** *sur`t·nihngs·mihd·duhl*
A glass of…, please.	**Et glass…, takk.** *eht glahs…tahk*
juice	**juice** *yews*
soda	**soda** *soo´·dah*
(sparkling/still) water	**vann (med kullsyre/uten kullsyre)** *vahn (meh kewl`·sui·ruh/ew`·tuhn kewl`·sui·ruh)*
Is the tap water safe to drink?	**Kan man drikke vann rett fra springen?** *kahn mahn drihk`·kuh vahn reht frah sprihng´·uhn*

Non-alcoholic Drinks

ananasjuice *ahn´·nah·nahs·yews*	pineapple juice
appelsinjuice *ahp·puhl·see´n·yews*	orange juice
brus *brews*	soda

If you're not in the mood for Norwegian beer or spirits, there are a number of other drinks to enjoy. Tea and especially strong coffee are commonly drunk throughout the day. For soft drinks you could try **Solo** (orange-flavored soda) or **Mozell** (apple-flavored soda).

YOU MAY HEAR...

Hva vil du ha å drikke? *vah vihl dew hah aw drihk`·kuh*
What would you like to drink?

Med eller uten kullsyre? *meh ehl´·luhr ew`·tuhn kewl`·sui·ruh*
Sparkling or still water?

eplesaft *eh`·pluh·sahft*	apple juice
grapefruktjuice *grehp´·frewkt·yews*	grapefruit juice
iste *ee`s·teh*	iced tea
lettmelk *leht´·mehlk*	low-fat milk
melk *mehlk*	milk

mineralvann med kullsyre/uten kullsyre *mih•nuh•rahl´•vahn meh kewl`•sui•ruh/ ew`•tuhn kewl`•sui•ruh*	sparkling/still mineral water
sitronbrus *siht•roo´n•brews*	lemonade

Aperitifs, Cocktails & Liqueurs

akevitt *ah•kuh•viht´*	aquavit
brandy *brehn´•dih*	brandy
gin tonic *dshihn tohn´•nihk*	gin and tonic
konjakk *kohn•yahk´*	cognac
likør *lih•kur´r*	liqueur
portvin *poort´•veen*	port
rom *rum*	rum
sherry *sher´•rih*	sherry
vermut *vehr´•mewt*	vermouth
vodka *vohd´•kah*	vodka
whisky *vihs´•kih*	whisky

Beer in Norway is classified by strength. **Lettøl** (beer with low alcohol content) is less than 2.5% alcohol content and **zero** and **vørterøl** are both non-alcoholic. **Pils** (lager) and **bayerøl** (medium-strength dark beer) are relatively low in alcohol content. The strongest beers (6-10%), like **eksportøl** (strong light beer) and **bokkøl** (strong dark beer), are only sold at the **Vinmonopolet** (state-run liquor store). If you are in Norway around Christmas time, be sure to try some of the special limited-edition Christmas brews which are extremely popular with the locals.

Beer, in addition to being drunk on its own, often serves as a chaser to **akevitt** (aquavit), an extremely potent drink distilled from potato and caraway seeds.

Beer

fatøl _fah`t·url_	draft [draught] beer
flaskeøl _flahs`·kuh·url_	bottled beer
lyst/mørkt øl _luist/murrkt url_	light/dark beer
pils _pihls_	lager
utenlandsk øl _ew`·tuhn·lahnsk url_	imported beer

Wine

avkjølt _ah´v·khurlt_	chilled
champagne _shahm·pahn´·yuh_	champagne
fyldig _fuil`·dih_	full-bodied
hvitvin _veet`·veen_	white
meget tørr _meh`·guht turr_	very dry
musserende _mews·seh´·ruh·nuh_	sparkling
rødvin _rur´·veen_	red
rosévin _roo·seh´·veen_	rosé
søt _surt_	sweet

On the Menu

abbor _ahb`·bohr_		perch
agurk _ah·gewr´k_		cucumber
akevitt _ah·kuh·viht´_		aquavit
akkar _ahk`·kahr_		squid
and _ahn_		duck
ananas _ahn´·nah·nahs_		pineapple
ananasjuice _ahn´·nah·nahs·yews_		pineapple juice
anisfrø _ah´·nihs·frur_		aniseed
ansjos _ahn·shoo´s_		anchovies or marinated sprat
appelsin _ahp·puhl·see´n_		orange
appelsinjuice _ahp·puhl·see´n·yews_		orange juice
appelsinmarmelade		orange marmalade
ahp·puhl·see´n·mahr·muh·lah·duh		
aprikos _ahp·rih·koo´s_		apricot
artisjokker _ar·tih·shohk´·kuhr_		artichokes
asparges _ahs·pahr´·guhs_		asparagus
aspargessuppe _ahs·pahr´·guhs·sewp·puh_		asparagus soup
aubergine _aw·buhr·shee´n_		eggplant [aubergine]
bacon _bay´·kuhn_		bacon
banan _bah·nah´n_		banana
basilikum _bah·see´·lih·kewm_		basil
benløse fugler _beh`n·lurs·uh few`l·uhr_		fried, rolled and stuffed slice of veal or beef
betasuppe _beh`·tah·sewp·puh_		thick meat and vegetable soup
biff _bihf_		beef steak
bjørnebær _byur`r·nuh·bar_		blackberries
blomkål _blohm´·kawl_		cauliflower
blomkålsuppe _blohm´·kawl·sewp·puh_		cauliflower soup

løtkake _blur`t_•*kah*•*kuh*	layer cake
låbær _blaw`_•*bar*	blueberries
låskjell _blaw`_•*shehl*	mussels
lekksprut _blehk`_•*sprewt*	octopus
randy _brehn´_•*dih*	brandy
rasme _brahs`_•*muh*	bream
rekkbønner _brehk´_•*burn*•*nuhr*	French beans
ringebær _brihng´_•*uh*•*bar*	raspberries
roiler _broi´_•*luhr*	chicken
rokkoli _brohk´_•*koh*•*lih*	broccoli
risling _brihs`_•*lihng*	sprat, brisling
run lapskaus *brewn* _lahps´_•*kevs*	Norwegian stew in brown gravy
rus *brews*	soda
rød *brur*	bread
uljong *bewl*•_yohng´_	consommé
ønner _burn`_•*nuhr*	beans
adler _dahd´_•*luhr*	dates
ill *dihl*	dill
ruer _drew`_•*uhr*	grapes
yrestek _dui`_•*ruh*•*stehk*	roast venison

egg *ehg*		eggs
eggerøre *ehg`·guh·rur·ruh*		scrambled eggs
einebær *ay`·nuh·bar*		juniper berries
ekte geitost *ehk`·tuh yayt`·ust*		goat cheese
elg *ehlg*		moose
elgbiff *ehlg`·bihf*		moose steak
elgfilet *ehlg`·fih·leh*		fillet of moose
elgstek *ehlg`·stehk*		roast moose
eple *ehp`·luh*		apple
eplekake *ehp`·luh·kah·kuh*		apple pie
eplesaft *eh`·pluh·sahft*		apple juice
erter *ehr´·tuhr*		peas
fasan *fah·sah´n*		pheasant
fatøl *fah`t·url*		draft [draught] beer
fenalår *feh`·nah·lawr*		cured leg of mutton
fersken *fehrs´·kuhn*		peach
fikener *fee`·kuhn·uhr*		figs
fisk *fihsk*		fish
fiskeboller *fihs`·kuh·bohl·luhr*		fish balls
fiskekabaret *fihs`·kuh·kah·bah·reh*		assorted seafood and vegetables in aspic
fiskepudding *fihs`·kuh·pewd·dihng*		fish pudding
fiskesuppe *fihs`·kuh·sewp·puh*		fish soup
flyndre *fluin`·druh*		flounder
fløtemysost *flur´·tuh·muis·ust*		mild and sweet cow's milk cheese
fransk løksuppe *frahnsk lur`k·sewp·puh*		French onion soup
frokostblanding *froo´·kohst·blahn·nihng*		cereal
fruktkompott *frewkt´·kohm·poht*		stewed fruit
fårekjøtt *faw`·ruh·khurt*		mutton
fårestek *faw`·ruh·stehk*		roast leg of mutton or lamb

fårikål _faw_ ´•rih•kawl	mutton or lamb in cabbage stew
gammelost _gahm_ `•muhl•ust	pungent cheese made with skimmed milk
gin tonic dshihn _tohn_ ´•nihk	gin and tonic
gjedde _yehd_ `•duh	pike
grapefrukt _grehp_ ´•frewkt	grapefruit
grapefruktjuice _grehp_ ´•frewkt•yews	grapefruit juice
gravlaks _grah_ `v•lahks	cured salmon flavored with dill
gresskar _grehs_ `•kahr	pumpkin
gressløk _grehs_ `•lurk	chives
grønnkål _grurn_ ´•kawl	kale
grønnsaksuppe _grurn_ `•sahk•sewp•puh	vegetable soup
gudbrandsdalsost _gewd_ `•brahns•dahls•ust	cow and goat's milk cheese
gul ertesuppe gewl _er_ `•tuh•sewp•puh	yellow pea soup
gulrøtter _gew_ `l•rurt•tuhr	carrots
gås gaws	goose
gåselever _gaw_ `•suh•leh•vuhr	goose liver
hare _hah_ `•ruh	hare
harestek _hah_ `•ruh•stehk	roast hare
hasselnøtter _hahs_ ´•suhl•nurt•tuhr	hazelnuts
havregrøt _hahv_ `•ruh•grurt	porridge
hellefisk _hehl_ ´•luh•fihsk	halibut
hjort yohrt	deer
hjortesadel _yohr_ `•tuh•sah•duhl	saddle of deer
hodesalat _hoo_ `•duh•sah•laht	lettuce
hoffdessert _hohf_ ´•dehs•sar	layers of meringue and whipped cream, topped with chocolate sauce and toasted almonds

honning _hohn`·nihng_	honey
hummer _hum´·muhr_	lobster
hvalbiff _vahl`·bihf_	whale steak
hvitløk _vee´t·lurk_	garlic
hvitting _viht`·tihng_	whiting
hvitvin _veet´·veen_	white wine
hyse _hui`·suh_	haddock (western Norway)
høne _hur`·nuh_	hen
ingefær _ihng´·uh·far_	ginger
is _ees_	ice cream
iste _ee`s·teh_	iced tea
jarlsbergost _yahrls´·behrg·ust_	mild, slightly sweet, semi-hard cheese
jordbær _yoor´·bar_	strawberries
juice _yews_	fruit juice
kaffe _kahf´·fuh_	coffee
kalkun _kahl·kew´n_	turkey
kalvebrissel _kahl`·vuh·brihs·suhl_	calf's sweetbread
kalvekjøtt _kahl`·vuh·khurt_	veal
kalvemedaljonger _kahl`·vuh·meh·dahl·yohng·uhr_	small round fillet of veal

alvelever _kahl`·vuh·lehv·vuhr_	calf's liver
amskjell _kahm`·shel_	scallop
anel _kah·neh´l_	cinnamon
anin _kah·nee´n_	rabbit
apers _kah´·puhrs_	capers
arbonade _kahr·bu·nah`·duh_	hamburger
arpe _kahr`·puh_	carp
astanjer _kahs·tahn´·yuhr_	chestnuts
arri _kahr´·rih_	curry seasoning
arve _kahr`·vuh_	caraway seeds
aviar _kah·vih·ah´r_	caviar
irsebær _khihr´·suh·bar_	cherries
jøttboller _khurt`·bohl·uhr_	meatballs
jøttkaker _khurt`·kahk·uhr_	small hamburgers
jøttpudding _khurt`·pud·dihng_	meatloaf
jøttsuppe _khurt`·sewp·puh_	meat soup
klippfisk _klihp´·fihsk_	salted and dried cod
noke _knoo`·kuh_	bone
okosnøtt _kuk´·kus·nurt_	coconut
olje _kohl`·yuh_	haddock (eastern Norway)
orinter _ku·rihn´·tuhr_	currants
otelett _koh·tuh·leht´_	chop
rabbe _krahb`·buh_	crab
reps _krehps_	freshwater crayfish
veite _kvay`·tuh_	halibut
ylling _khuil`·lihng_	chicken
ål _kawl_	cabbage
ålrabi/kålrot _kawl·rah´·bih/kawl`·root_	rutabaga [swede BE]
antareller _kahn·tah·rehl´·luhr_	chanterelle mushrooms
aramellpudding _kah·rah·mehl´·pewd·dihng_	creme caramel
okte poteter _kuk`·tuh pu·teh´t·uhr_	boiled potatoes

komler/komper _kum`_•luhr/_kum`_•puhr	potato dumplings (western Norway)
konjakk kohn•_yahk´_	cognac
krem kr_eh_m	whipped cream
laks lahks	salmon
lammebog _lahm`_•muh•b_oo_g	shoulder of lamb
lammebryst _lahm`_•muh•br_ui_st	brisket of lamb
lammekjøtt _lahm`_•muh•kh_ur_t	lamb
lammelår _lahm`_•muh•l_aw_r	leg of lamb
lammesadel _lahm`_•muh•**sah**•duhl	saddle of lamb
lammestek _lahm`_•muh•st_eh_k	roast lamb
lapskaus _lahps´_•kevs	Norwegian stew with meat potatoes and vegetables
lettmelk _leht`_•mehlk	low-fat milk
lever _lehv´_•vuhr	liver
likør lih•_kur´r_	liqueur
linser _lihn`_•suhr	lentils
lungemos _lung`_•uh•m_oo_s	ground [minced] lungs and onions
lutefisk _lew`_•tuh•fihsk	stockfish soaked in lye
lys lapskaus _lui_s _lahps´_•kevs	Norwegian stew with diced, salted and boiled pork
løk _lur_k	onions
løksuppe _lur`_k•sewp•puh	onion soup
mais mies	corn
maiskolbe _mies´_•kohl•buh	corn on the cob
mandarin mahn•dah•_ree´n_	tangerine
mandelkake _mahn´_•duhl•k_ah_•kuh	almond cake
mandler _mahn´d_•luhr	almonds
makrell mahk•_rehl´_	mackerel
markjordbær _mahr`_k•_yoor_•bar	wild strawberries

nedisterkaker *meh·<u>dihs</u>´·tuhr·**kah**·kuhr*	small pork and beef hamburgers
nedisterpølse *meh·<u>dihs</u>´·tuhr·purl·suh*	pork and beef sausage
nelk *mehlk*	milk
nelon *meh·<u>loo</u>´n*	melon
nilkshake <u>mihlk</u>´·shayk	milkshake
nineralvann *mih·nuh·<u>rahl</u>´·vahn*	mineral water
nolter/multer <u>mohl</u>´·tuhr/<u>mewl</u>´·tuhr	arctic cloudberries
noreller *mu·<u>rehl</u>´·luhr*	morello cherries
nørbradstek *<u>mur</u>´r·brahd·stehk*	roast sirloin
ektarin *nehk·tah·<u>ree</u>´n*	nectarine
ellik <u>nehl</u>´·lihk	clove
eslesuppe <u>nehs</u>´·luh·sewp·puh	nettle soup
epe <u>neh</u>`·puh	turnip
ormannaost *noor·<u>mahn</u>´·nah·ust*	blue-veined cow's milk cheese
udler <u>newd</u>´·luhr	noodles
ypoteter <u>nui</u>`·pu·**teht**·uhr	new potatoes
yrer <u>nui</u>`·ruhr	kidneys
øtter <u>nurt</u>´·tuhr	nuts
ksebryst <u>ohk</u>`·suh·bruist	brisket of beef
ksefilet <u>ohk</u>`·suh·fih·**leh**	fillet of beef

oksehalesuppe _ohk`·suh·hah·luh·sewp·puh_	oxtail soup
oksekam _ohk`·suh·kahm_	loin
oksekjøtt _ohk`·suh·khurt_	beef
okserulader _ohk`·suh·rewl·lah·duhr_	braised beef rolls
oksestek _ohk`·suh·stehk_	roast beef
omelett _oh·muh·leht´_	omelet
orrfugl _ohr`·fewl_	black grouse, a woodland b
ost _ust_	cheese
pannekaker _pahn`·nuh·kah·kuhr_	pancakes
paprika _pahp´·rih·kah_	sweet pepper
peanøtter _pee´·ah·nurt·tuhr_	peanuts
pepper _pehp´·puhr_	pepper
persille _pehr·sihl`·luh_	parsley
piggvar _pihg`·vahr_	turbot
pils _pihls_	lager
pinnekjøtt _pihn`·nuh·khurt_	salted and dried mutton rib
	steamed on twigs
plommer _plum`·muhr_	plums
pommes frites _pohm friht_	French fries [chips]
portvin _poort´·veen_	port wine
potet _pu·teh´t_	potato

potetgull _pu·**teh**´t·gewl_	potato chips [crisps]
potetkroketter _pu·**teh**´t·krohk·keht·tuhr_	potato croquettes
potetmos _pu·**teh**´t·moos_	mashed potatoes
potetsalat _pu·**teh**´t·sah·**laht**_	potato salad
purre _**pewr**`·ruh_	leeks
pølse _**purl**`·suh_	sausage
pære _**pa**`·ruh_	pear
pære Belle Helene _**pa**`·ruh behl heh·**leh**´n_	poached pears with vanilla ice cream and chocolate
rabarbra _rah·**bahr**´·brah_	rhubarb
rakørret _**rah**´k·urr·ruht_	salt-cured and fermented trout
raspeball _**rahs**`·puh·bahl_	potato dumplings
reddiker _**rehd**´·dihk·kuhr_	radishes
regnbueørret _**rayn**`·bew·uh·urr·ruht_	rainbow trout
rekecocktail _**reh**`·kuh·kohk·tayl_	shrimp [prawn] cocktail
reker _**reh**`·kuhr_	shrimp [prawns]
rips _rihps_	red currants
ris _rees_	rice
ristet brød _**rihs**`·tuht brur_	toast
rogn _rohngn_	roe
rognebær _**rohng**`·nuh·bar_	rowanberries
rosenkål _**roo**´·suhn·kawl_	Brussels sprouts
rosiner _ru·**see**´·nuhr_	raisins
rundstykke _**rewn**´·stuik·kuh_	roll
rødbeter _**rur**´·beh·tuhr_	beet [beetroot]
rødkål _**rur**´·kawl_	red cabbage
rødspette _**rur**`·speht·tuh_	plaice
røkelaks _**rur**`·kuh·lahks_	smoked salmon
røye _**rury**`·uh_	char
rådyr _**raw**´·duir_	roe-deer

Wolffish
Monkfish
Filet of reindeer
Whalesteak

rådyrsadel _raw´·duir·sah·duhl_ — saddle of venison

rådyrstek _raw´·duir·stehk_ — roast venison

ragu _rah·gew´_ — ragout

rapphøne _rahp`·hur·nuh_ — partridge

reinsdyr _rayns´·duir_ — reindeer

reinsdyrmedaljonger _rayns´·duir·meh·dahl·yohng·uhr_ — small, round fillets of reinde

reinsdyrstek _rayns´·duir·stehk_ — roast reindeer

ribbe _rihb`·buh_ — spareribs

ridderost _rihd´·duhr·ust_ — semi-hard cheese with nutt flavor

riskrem _ree´s·krehm_ — creamed rice with red berry sauce

roastbiff _rohst´·bihf_ — broiled steak

rom _rum_ — rum

rosévin _roo·seh´·veen_ — rosé wine

rype _rui´·puh_ — grouse, a mountain bird

rødgrøt med fløte _rur`·grurt meh flur`·tuh_ — berry compote with cream

rødvin _rur´·veen_ — red wine

salat _sah·lah´t_ — salad

salt _sahlt_ — salt

altkjøttlapskaus _sahlt`·khurt·lahps´·kevs_ — Norwegian stew with diced, salted and boiled pork

alvie _sahl·vee`·uh_ — sage

ardell _sar·dehl´_ — canned anchovy

ardin _sar·dee´n_ — sardine

ei _say_ — pollock

elleri _sehl·luhr·ee´_ — celery

ellerisuppe _seh·luh·ree´·sewp·puh_ — celery soup

herry _sher´·rih_ — sherry

ik _seek_ — whitefish

ild _sihl_ — herring

ildeball _sihl`·luh·bahl_ — potato dumplings filled with minced salted herring

itron _siht·roo´n_ — lemon

itronbrus _siht·roo´n·brews_ — lemonade

jampinjonger _sham·pihn·yohng´·uhr_ — button mushrooms

jampinjongsuppe _hahm·pihn·yohng´·sewp·puh_ — button mushroom soup

jokoladepudding _hu·ku·lah`·duh·pewd·dihng_ — chocolate pudding

jømat _shur`·maht_ — seafood

jøørret _shur`·urr·ruht_ — sea trout

jøtunge _shur`·tung·uh_ — sole

kalldyr _skahl`·duir_ — shellfish

kinke _shihng`·kuh_ — ham

lettvar _sleht`·vahr_ — brill

mør _smurr_ — butter

olbær _soo´l·bar_ — black currants

opp _sohp_ — mushrooms

orbett _sohr·beht´_ — sorbet

pinat _spih·nah´t_ — spinach

steinbit _stayn`_·beet	catfish
stek _stehk_	roast
stekte poteter _stehk`_·tuh _pu·teh´t_·uhr	sautéed potatoes
stikkelsbær _stihk`_·kuhls·bar	gooseberries
stuede poteter _stew`_·eh·duh _pu·teh´t_·uhr	potatoes in a white sauce
stør _sturr_	sturgeon
størje _sturr`_·yuh	tuna
sufflé _sewf·leh´_	soufflé
surkål _sew´r_·kawl	coleslaw
sursild _sew´r_·sihl	marinated herring
svinefilet _svee`_·nuh·fih·leh	fillet of pork
svinekam _svee`_·nuh·kahm	loin of pork
svinekjøtt _svee`_·nuh·khurt	pork
svinestek _svee`_·nuh·stehk	roast pork
svisker _svihs`_·kuhr	prunes
svor _svoor_	bacon rind [crackling]
sylte _suil`_·tuh	head cheese [brawn]
sylteagurk _suil`_·tuh·ah·gewrk	pickled gherkin
syltetøy _suil`_·tuh·tury	jam
tartarbiff _tahr·tah´r_·bihf	steak tartare
T-benstek _teh´_·behn·stehk	T-bone steak
te _teh_	tea
terte _tehr`_·tuh	fruit cake
tilslørte bondepiker _tihl´_·slurr·tuh	layers of stewed apples,
bun´·nuh·pee·kuhr	cookie [biscuit] crumbs and
	whipped cream
timian _tee´_·mih·ahn	thyme
tomater _tu·maht´_·uhr	tomatoes
tomatsuppe _tu·mah´t_·sewp·puh	tomato soup
torsk _tohrsk_	cod
tranebær _trah`_·nuh·bar	cranberries
tunfisk _tew´n_·fihsk	tuna

tunge _tung`_•uh	tongue
tyttebær _tuit´_•tuh•bar	lingonberry
tørrfisk _turr´_•fihsk	stockfish
uer _ew`_•uhr	rosefish (seafood)
vafler _vahf´_•luhr	waffles
vaktel _vahk´_•tuhl	quail
valnøtter _vahl`_•nurt•tuhr	walnuts
vaniljesaus vah•_nihl`_•yuh•sevs	vanilla sauce
vannmelon _vahn`_•meh•_loon_	watermelon
varm sjokolade vahrm shu•ku•_lah`_•duh	hot chocolate
vermut _vehr´_•mewt	vermouth
villand _vihl`_•lahn	wild duck
vin veen	wine
vodka _vohd´_•kah	vodka
whisky _vihs´_•kih	whisky
wienerschnitzel _vee´_•nuhr•shniht•suhl	breaded veal cutlet
yoghurt _yoo´_•gewrt	yogurt
øl url	beer
ørret _urr`_•ruht	trout
østers _urs´_•tehrs	oysters
åbor _aw`_•bohr	perch
ål awl	eel

People

ESSENTIAL

Hello/Hi!	**Hallo/Hei!** *hah·loo´/hay*
How are you?	**Hvordan står det til?** *voor´·dahn stawr deh tihl*
Fine, thanks.	**Bare bra, takk.** *bah`·ruh brah tahk*
Excuse me.	**Unnskyld.** *ewn´·shewl*
Do you speak English?	**Snakker du engelsk?** *snahk`·kuhr dew ehng´·ehlsk*
What's your name?	**Hva heter du?** *vah heh`·tuhr dew*
My name is...	**Jeg heter...** *yay heh`·tuhr...*
Nice to meet you!	**Hyggelig å treffes!** *huig`·guh·lih aw trehf´·fuhs*
Where are you from?	**Hvor kommer du fra?** *voor kohm´·muhr dew frah*
I'm from the U.S./ the U.K.	**Jeg er fra USA/Storbritannia.** *yay ar frah ew·ehs·ah´/stoo´r·brih·tahn·yah*
What do you do?	**Hva jobber du med?** *vah yohb`·buhr dew meh*
I work for...	**Jeg jobber for...** *yay yohb`·buhr fohr...*
I'm a student.	**Jeg er student.** *yay ar stew·dehnt´*
I'm retired.	**Jeg er pensjonist.** *yay ar pang·shu·nihst´*
Do you like...?	**Liker du...?** *lee´·kuhr dew...*
Goodbye.	**Adjø.** *ahd·yur´*
See you later.	**Vi ses.** *vee seh`·uhs*

Language Difficulties

Do you speak English?	**Snakker du engelsk?** *snahk`·kuhr dew ehng´·uhlsk*
Does anyone here speak English?	**Er det noen her som snakker engelsk?** *ar deh noo`·uhn har sohm snahk`·kuhr ehng´·uhlsk*
I don't speak (much) Norwegian.	**Jeg snakker ikke (så bra) norsk.** *yay snahk`·kuhr ihk`·kuh (saw brah) norsk*

De (the formal form of 'you') is generally no longer used to address strangers, but is restricted to written works and addressing older people. As a general rule, **du** can be used in all situations without offending anyone.

Could you speak more slowly?	**Kan du snakke litt langsommere?** *kahn dew snahk`•kuh liht lahng`•sohm•muh•ruh*
Could you repeat that?	**Kan du gjenta det?** *kahn dew yehn´•tah deh*
Excuse me.	**Unnskyld.** *ewn´•shewl*
What was that?	**Hva sa du?** *vah sah dew*
Can you write it down?	**Kan du skrive det?** *kahn dew skree`•vuh deh*
Can you translate this for me?	**Kan du oversette dette for meg?** *kahn dew aw`•vuhr•seht•tuh deht`•tuh fohr may*
What does this mean?	**Hva betyr dette?** *vah buh•tui´r deht`•tuh*
I (don't) understand.	**Jeg forstår (ikke).** *yay for•staw´r (ihk`•kuh)*
Do you understand?	**Forstår du?** *for•staw´r dew*

YOU MAY HEAR...

Jeg snakker ikke engelsk.
yay snahk`•kuhr ihk`•kuh ehng´•uhlsk

I don't speak English.

Jeg snakker bare litt engelsk. *yay sahk•ehr bahr•eh liht ehn•gehlsk*

I only speak a little English.

Making Friends

Hello/Hi!	**Hallo/Hei!** *hah•loo´/hay*
Good morning.	**God morgen.** *gum•maw`•ruhn*
Good afternoon.	**God dag.** *gud•dah´g*
Good evening.	**God aften/God kveld.** *gu•ahf´•tuhn/guk•kvehl´*
My name is...	**Jeg heter...** *yay heh`•tuhr...*
Can I introduce you to...?	**Kan jeg få presentere deg for...?** *kahn yay faw pre•sahng•teh´•ruh day fohr...*
Nice to meet you!	**Hyggelig å treffes!** *huig´•guh•lih oh trehf`•fuhs*
How are you?	**Hvordan står det til?** *voor´•dahn stawr deh tihl*
Fine, thanks.	**Bare bra, takk.** *bah`•ruh brah tahk*
And you?	**Og med deg?** *oh meh day*

Travel Talk

I'm here...	**Jeg er her...** *yay ar har...*
on business	**i forretninger** *ih fohr•reht´•nihng•uhr*
on vacation [holiday]	**på ferie** *poh feh´r•yuh*
studying	**som student** *sohm stew•dehn´t*
I'm staying for...	**Jeg blir her...** *yay bleer har...*
I've been here...	**Jeg har vært her...** *yay hahr vehrt har...*
a day	**en dag** *ehn dahg*
a week	**en uke** *ehn ew`•kuh*
a month	**en måned** *ehn maw´•nuhd*

Where are you from?	**Hvor kommer du fra?** *voor <u>kohm</u>´-muhr dew frah*
I'm from...	**Jeg er fra...** *yay ar frah...*

For Numbers, see page 170.

Personal

Who are you with?	**Hvem reiser du sammen med?** *vehm <u>ray</u>`-suhr dew <u>sahm</u>´-muhn meh*
I'm on my own.	**Jeg reiser alene.** *yay <u>ray</u>`-suhr ah-<u>leh</u>`-nuh*
I'm with...	**Jeg er her med...** *yay ar har meh...*
my husband/wife	**mannen min/kona mi** *<u>mahn</u>´-nuhn mihn/<u>koo</u>`-na mih*
my boyfriend/ girlfriend	**kjæresten min** *<u>kha</u>`-reh-stuhn mihn*
a friend	**en venn** *ehn vehn*
a colleague	**en kollega** *ehn kohl-<u>leh</u>´-gah*
colleagues	**kolleger** *kul·ehg·ehr*
When's your birthday?	**Når har du bursdag?** *nohr <u>hahr</u> dew <u>bew</u>´rs-dahg*
How old are you?	**Hvor gammel er du?** *voor <u>gahm</u>`-muhl ar dew*
I'm...	**Jeg er...** *yay ar...*
Are you married?	**Er du gift?** *ar dew yihft*
I'm...	**Jeg er...** *yay ar...*
single	**ugift** *<u>ew</u>`-yihft*
in a relationship	**opptatt** *<u>ohp</u>`-taht*
engaged	**Jeg er forlovet** *yay ar fawr·lawv·eht*
married	**gift** *yihft*
divorced	**skilt** *shihlt*
separated	**separert** *seh·pah·<u>reh</u>´rt*
I'm widowed.	**Jeg er enkemann** *m* **/enke** *f.* *yay ar <u>ehng</u>`·kuh·mahn/<u>ehng</u>`·kuh*

Do you have children/ grandchildren? | **Har du barn/barnebarn?** _hahr_ dew bahrn/ _bah`rn•uh•bahrn_

For Numbers, see page 170.

Work & School

What do you do?	**Hva jobber du med?** vah _yohb`•buhr_ dew meh
What are you studying?	**Hva studerer du?** vah stew•_deh´•ruhr_ dew
I'm studying...	**Jeg studerer...** yay stew•_deh´•ruhr..._
I work full time/ part time.	**Jeg jobber fulltid/deltid.** yay _yohb`•bur_ _fewl´•teed/ dehl´•teed_
I am unemployed.	**Jeg er arbeidsledig.** yay ar ahr•bayds•leh•dihg
I work at home.	**Jeg jobber hjemmefra.** yay jawb•ehr yem•eh•frah
Who do you work for?	**Hvem jobber du for?** vehm _yohb`•buhr_ dew fohr
I work for...	**Jeg jobber for...** yay _yohb`•buhr_ fohr...
Here's my business card.	**Her er visittkortet mitt.** har ar vihs•_iht´_•kor•tuh miht

For Business Travel, see page 144.

Weather

What's the weather forecast?	**Hva sier værmeldingen?** *vah see`·uhr var`·mehl·lihng·uhn*
What beautiful weather!	**Så fint vær det er!** *soh feent var deh ar*
What terrible weather!	**For et forferdelig vær!** *fohr eht fohr·fehr´·duh·lih v...*
It's cool/warm.	**Det er kjølig/varmt.** *deh ar khur`·lih/vahrmt*
It's snowy/icy.	**Det snør/er kaldt.** *deh snurr/ar kahlt*
It's rainy.	**Det regner.** *deh rayn`·uhr*
It's sunny.	**Sola skinner.** *soo´·lah shih´·nuhr*
Do I need a jacket/ an umbrella?	**Trenger jeg jakke/paraply?** *trehng´·uhr yay yahk`·kuh/pah·rah·plui´*

For Temperature, see page 176.

ESSENTIAL

Would you like to go out for a drink/meal?	**Skal vi gå og ta en drink/ut og spise?** *skahl vee gaw oh tah ehn dringk/ewt oh spee`•suh*
What are your plans for tonight/tomorrow?	**Hva gjør du i kveld/i morgen?** *vah yurr dew ih kvehl/ih maw`•ruhn*
Can I have your number?	**Kan jeg få nummeret ditt?** *kahn yay faw num´•muhr•uh diht*
Can I join you?	**Er det opptatt her?** *ar deh awp•that har*
Can I buy you a drink?	**Kan jeg by på en drink?** *kahn yay bui poh ehn drihngk*
I like you.	**Jeg liker deg.** *yay lee´•kuhr day*
I love you.	**Jeg elsker deg.** *yay ehls`•kuhr day*

The Dating Game

Would you like to go out for coffee?	**Skal vi gå og ta en kaffe?** *skahl vee gaw oh tah ehn kahf´•fuh*
Would you like to go out for a drink/ for dinner?	**Har du lyst å ta en drink/gå og spise middag?** *hahr dew lyst aw tah ehn drihnk/gaw awg spih•seh mihd•ahg*
What are your plans for…?	**Hva gjør du…?** *vah yurr dew…*
tonight	**i kveld** *ih kvehl*
tomorrow	**i morgen** *ih maw`•ruhn*
this weekend	**i helgen** *ih hehl´•guhn*
Where would you like to go?	**Hvor vil du dra?** *voor vihl dew drah*
I'd like to go to…	**Jeg vil gjerne dra til…** *yay vihl ya`r•nuh drah tihl…*

Do you like...?	**Liker du...?** _lee´·kuhr d__ew_...
Can I have your number/e−mail?	**Kan jeg få nummeret ditt/e-postadressen din?** _kahn yay faw _num´·muh·ruh diht/_eh´·pohst·ahd·rehs·suhn dihn_
Are you on Facebook/Twitter?	**Er du på Facebook/Twitter?** _Ar dew paw feis·bewk_ tviht·ehr
Can I join you?	**Kan jeg slå meg ned her?** _kahn yay slaw may nehd har_
You're very attractive.	**Du er svært tiltrekkende.** _dew ar svart __tihl´·trehk·kuhn·uh_
Should we go somewhere quieter?	**Skal vi gå til et roligere sted?** _skahl vee gaw tihl et __roo`·lih·uh·ruh stehd_

For Communications, see page 49.

Accepting & Rejecting

I'd love to, thanks.	**Takk, det vil jeg gjerne.** _tahk deh vihl yay ya´r·nuh_
Where should we meet?	**Hvor skal vi møtes?** _voor skahl vee __mur`·tuhs_
Let's meet at the bar/your hotel.	**Vi møtes i baren/på hotellet ditt.** _vee __mur`·tuhs i_ bah´·ruhn/poh hu·tehl´·luh diht
I'll come by at...	**Jeg henter deg...** _yay __hehn`·tuhr day_...

What's your address?	**Hva er adressen din?**	vah ar ahd•_rehs_´•suhn dihn
Thanks, but I'm busy.	**Takk, men jeg er dessverre opptatt.**	tahk mehn yay ar dehs•_vehr_´•ruh ohp´•taht
I'm not interested.	**Jeg er ikke interessert.**	yay ar _ihk_`•kuh ihn•truhs•_seh_´rt
Leave me alone.	**Vær så snill å la meg være i fred.**	var soh snihl oh lah may _va_`•ruh ih freh
Stop bothering me!	**Slutt å plage meg!**	slewt oh _plah_`•guh may

For Time, see page 171.

Getting Intimate

Can I hug/kiss you?	**Kan jeg holde rundt/kysse deg?**	kahn yay _hohl_`•luh rewnt/_khuis_`•suh day
Yes.	**Ja.**	yah
No.	**Nei.**	nay
Stop!	**Stopp!**	stohp
I love you.	**Jeg elsker deg.**	yay _ehls_`•kuhr day

Sexual Preferences

Are you gay?	**Er du homofil?**	ar dew hu•mu•_fee_´l
I'm...	**Jeg er...**	yay ar...
heterosexual	**heterofil**	heh•teh•ru•_fee_´l
homosexual	**homofil**	hu•mu•_fee_´l
bisexual	**bifil**	bih•_fee_´l
Do you like men/women?	**Liker du menn/kvinner?**	_lee_´•kuhr dew mehn/_kvihn_`•nuhr

Leisure Time

ESSENTIAL

Where's the tourist information office?	**Hvor er turistkontoret?** *voor ar tew-rihst´-kun-too-ruh*
What are the main points of interest?	**Hva er de viktigste severdighetene?** *vah ar dih vihk`-tik-stuh seh-vehr´-dih-heh-tuh-nuh*
Do you have tours in English?	**Har dere omvisninger på engelsk?** *hahr deh`-ruh ohm´-vihs-nihng-uhr poh ehng´-uhlsk*
Can I have a map/guide?	**Kan jeg få et kart/en guide?** *kahn yay faw eht kahrt/ehn gied*

Tourist Information

Do you have any information on…?	**Har dere informasjon om…?** *hahr deh`-ruh ihn-fohr-mah-shoo´n ohm…*
Can you recommend…?	**Kan dere anbefale…?** *kahn deh`-ruh ahn´-buh-fah-luh…*
a boat trip	**en båttur** *ehn bawt`-tewr*
an excursion	**en utflukt** *ehn ew`t-flewkt*
a sightseeing tour	**en sightseeingtur** *ehn siet´-see-ihng-tewr*

Tourist offices are located throughout Norway. The local tourist office can provide information for visitors on accommodation, activities and other entertainment. Visit Norway, the official website of the Norwegian Tourist Board, www.visitnorway.com, can provide information about locations in particular cities.

On Tour

I'd like to go on the tour to…	**Jeg vil gjerne bli med på turen til…** *yay vihl ya`r•nuh blih meh poh <u>tew´</u>•ruhn tihl…*
When's the next tour?	**Når går neste tur?** *nohr gawr <u>nehs</u>`•tuh tewr*
Are there tours in English?	**Fins det turer på engelsk?** *fihns deh <u>tew´</u>r•uhr poh <u>ehng´</u>•uhlsk*
Is there an English-speaking guide/an audio guide in English?	**Fins det en engelsktalende guide/en lydguide på engelsk?** *fihns deh ehn <u>ehng´</u>•uhlsk•<u>tah</u>l•uhn•uh gied/ehn <u>luid`</u>•gied poh <u>ehng´</u>•uhlsk*
What time do we leave?	**Når drar vi?** *nohr drahr vee*
What time do we return?	**Når kommer vi tilbake?** *nohr <u>kohm´</u>•muhr vee tihl•<u>bah</u>`•kuh*
We'd like to see…	**Vi vil gjerne se på…** *vee vihl <u>ya`</u>r•nuh seh poh…*
Can we stop here…?	**Kan vi stoppe her…?** *kahn vee <u>stohp</u>`•puh har…*
to take photographs	**for å ta bilder** *fohr oh <u>tah</u> <u>bihl´</u>•duhr*
to buy souvenirs	**for å kjøpe suvenirer** *fohr oh <u>khur´</u>•puh sew•vuh•<u>nee´</u>r•uhr*
to use the restroom [toilet]	**for å gå på toalettet** *forh oh gaw poh tu•ah•<u>leh´</u>•tuh*

s it disabled-ccessible?	**Er det adkomst for bevegelseshemmede?** *ar deh ahd`·kohmst fohr buh·veh´·guhl·suhs·hem·muhd·uh*

or Tickets, see page 20.

eeing the Sights

Where is/are...?	**Hvor er...?** *voor ar...*
the battleground	**slagstedet** *slah`g·steh·duh*
the botanical gardens	**den botaniske hagen** *dehn bu·tah´·nihsk·uh hah`·guhn*
the castle	**slottet** *slot´·tuh*
the downtown area	**sentrum** *sehn´·trewm*
the fair	**markedet** *mahr`·kehd·uh*
the fortress	**festningen** *fehst`·nihng·uhn*
the fountain	**fontenen** *fon·teh`·nuhn*
the library	**biblioteket** *bihb·lyu·teh´·kuh*
the market	**torget** *tohr´·guh*
the museum	**museet** *mew·seh´·uh*
the old town	**gamlebyen** *gahm`·luh·bui·uhn*
the palace	**slottet** *slot´·tuh*
the park	**parken** *pahr´·kuhn*

the ruins	**ruinene** *rew•ee´n•uh•nuh*
the shopping area	**handlestrøket** *hahn`d•luh•strur•kuh*
the town square	**rådhusplassen** *rawd`•hews•plah•suhn*
Can you show me on the map?	**Kan du vise meg på kartet hvor jeg er?** *kahn dew vee`•suh may paw kahr´•tuh voor yay ar*
It's...	**Det er...** *deh ar...*
amazing	**praktfullt** *prahkt`•fewlt*
beautiful	**vakkert** *vahk´•kuhrt*
boring	**kjedelig** *kheh`•duh•lih*
interesting	**interessant** *ihn•tuh•rehs•sahng´t*
magnificent	**storslagent** *stoo`r•slahg•uhnt*
romantic	**romantisk** *ru•mahn´•tihsk*
strange	**underlig** *ewn`•dur•lih*
stunning	**overveldende** *aw`•vuhr•vehl•duhn•uh*
terrible	**forferdelig** *fohr•fa´r•duh•lih*
ugly	**stygt** *stuikt*
I (don't) like it.	**Jeg liker det (ikke).** *yay lee´•kuhr deh (ihk`•kuh)*

For Asking Directions, see page 34.

Religious Sites

Where's...?	**Hvor er...?** _voor ar..._
the cathedral	**domkirken** _dohm´•khihr•kuhn_
the church	**kirken** _khihr`•kuhn_
the mosque	**moskéen** _mus•keh´•uhn_
the synagogue	**synagogen** _sui•nah•goo`•guhn_
the temple	**templet** _tehm´p•luh_
What time is mass/ the service?	**Når begynner messen/gudstjenesten?** _nohr buh•yuin´•nuhr mehs`•suhn/gewds`•tyeh•nuhs•tuhn_

Shopping

ESSENTIAL

Where is the market/ mall [shopping centre]?	**Hvor er torget/kjøpesenteret?** _voor ar tohr´•guh/ khur`•puh•sehn•truh_
I'm just looking.	**Jeg bare ser meg omkring.** _yay bah`•ruh sehr may ohm•krihng´_
Can you help me?	**Kan du hjelpe meg?** _kahn dew yehl´•puh may_
I'm being helped.	**Jeg får hjelp.** _yay fawr yehlp_
How much?	**Hvor mye koster det?** _voor mew`•uh kohs`•tuhr deh_
That one.	**Den der.** _dehn dar_
No, thanks. That's all.	**Nei takk. Det var alt.** _nay tahk deh vahr ahlt_
Where do I pay?	**Hvor betaler man?** _voor buh•tah´•luhr mahn_
I'll pay in cash/by credit card.	**Jeg betaler kontant/med kredittkort.** _yay buh•tah´•luhr kun•tahn´t/meh kreh•diht´•kohrt_
Could I have a receipt?	**Kan jeg få kvittering?** _kahn yay faw kviht•teh´•rihng_

YOU MAY SEE...

UTE TIL LUNSJ	closed for lunch
BETAL HER	pay here
VI TAR KREDITTKORT	credit cards accepted
ÅPNINGSTIDER	opening hours

At the Shops

Where is...?	**Hvor er det...?** *voor ar deh...*
the antiques store	**en antikvitetshandel** *ehn ahn·tih·kvih·teh´ts·hahn·duhl*
the bakery	**et bakeri** *eht bah·kuhr·ee´*
the bank	**en bank** *ehn bahngk*
the bookstore	**en bokhandel** *ehn book`·hahn·duhl*
the clothing store	**en klesbutikk** *ehn kleh`s·bew·tihk*
the delicatessen	**en delikatesseforretning** *ehn deh·lih·kah·tehs´·suh·fohr·reht·nihng*
the department store	**et stormagasin** *eht stoor`·mah·gah·seen*
the gift shop	**en gavebutikk** *ehn gah`·vuh·bew·tihk*

Norway offers shopping choices for a range of budgets. Even in
the capital, a good deal of shopping can be done on foot. Many
of the major stores are located in the area around **Karl Johans** gate
and on **Bogstadveien** and **Hegdehaugsveien** streets. **Grünerløkka**
is the place to go to find trendy boutiques showcasing the work of
young Norwegian designers. Here you'll also find lots of second-hand
shops, music stores and independent stores selling local pottery and
handicrafts. For everything under one roof in Oslo, visit **Aker Brygge**,
Byporten, **Glasmagasinet**, **Oslo City**, **Paleet**, **Steen & Strøm** and
Vikaterrassen.

Regular store hours are Monday to Friday from 9:00 a.m. to 5:00 p.m. (on
Saturday to 3:00 p.m.), but many stores stay open later. Shopping malls
are generally open Monday to Friday from 10:00 a.m. to 9:00 p.m. and
Saturday from 9:00 a.m. to 6:00 p.m. Most stores are closed on Sunday.

the health food store	**en helsekostbutikk** *ehn hehl`·suh·kohst·fohr·reht·nihng*
the jeweler	**en gullsmed** *ehn gewl`·smeh*
the liquor store [off-licence]	**et vinmonopol** *eht vee`n·mu·nu·pool*
the market	**et torg** *eht tohrg*
the music store	**musikkforretningen** *mews·ihk·fawr·eht·nihng·ehn*
the pastry shop	**et konditori** *eht kun·dih·tu·ree´*
the pharmacy [chemist]	**et apotek** *eht ah·pu·teh´k*
the produce [grocery] store	**en matvarebutikk** *ehn mah`t·vah·ruh·bew·tihk*
the shoe store	**en skoforretning** *ehn skoo´·fohr·reht´·nihng*
the shopping mall	**et butikksenter** *eht bew·tihk´·sehn·tuhr*
the souvenir store	**en suvenirbutikk** *ehn sew·vuh·nee´r·bew·tihk*

YOU MAY HEAR...

Kan jeg hjelpe deg? *kahn yay* *yehl`•puh day* — Can I help you?

Et øyeblikk. *eht ury`•uh•blihk* — One moment.

Hva skal det være? *vah skahl deh va`•ruh* — What would you like?

Skal det være noe annet? *skahl deh va`•ruh noo`•uh ahn`•nuht* — Anything else?

Where is...?	**Hvor er det...?** *voor ar deh...*
the supermarket	**et supermarked** *eht sew`•puhr•mahr•kuhd*
the tobacconist	**en tobakksbutikk** *ehn tu•bahk´s•bew•tihk*
the toy store	**en leketøysbutikk** *ehn leh`•kuh•turys•bew•tihk*

Ask an Assistant

When do you open/close?	**Når åpner/stenger dere?** *nawr åwpn•er/stehng•ehr dehr•eh*
When does... open/close?	**Når åpner/stenger...?** *nohr aw`p•nuhr/stehng`•uhr...*
Where is...?	**Hvor er...?** *voor ar...*
the cash desk	**kassen** *kahs`•suhn*
the escalator	**rulletrappen** *rewl`•luh•trahp•puhn*
the elevator [lift]	**heisen** *hay´•suhn*
the fitting room	**prøverommet** *prur`•vuh•rum•muh*
the store directory [guide]	**butikkguiden** *bew•tihk´•gie•duhn*
Can you help me?	**Kan du hjelpe meg?** *kahn dew yehl`•puh may*
I'm just looking.	**Jeg bare ser meg omkring.** *yay bah`•ruh sehr may ohm•krihng´*
I'm being helped.	**Jeg får hjelp.** *yay fawr yehlp*

Do you have anything in…?	**Har du noe i…?** _hahr dew <u>noo</u>`•uh ih…_	
Can you show me…?	**Kan du vise meg…?** _kahn dew <u>vee</u>`•suh may…_	
Can you ship/wrap it?	**Kan du sende den/pakke den inn?** _kahn dew <u>seh</u>`•nuh dehn/<u>pahk</u>`•kuh dehn ihn_	
How much?	**Hvor mye koster det?** _voor <u>mui</u>`•uh <u>kohs</u>`•tuhr deh_	
That's all.	**Det var alt.** _deh var ahlt_	

For Clothing, see page 124.

For Souvenirs, see page 130.

Personal Preferences

I'd like something…	**Jeg vil gjerne ha noe…** _yay vihl <u>ya</u>`•nuh hah <u>noo</u>`•uh…_	
cheap/expensive	**billig/dyrt** _<u>bihl</u>`•lih/d<u>ui</u>rt_	
larger/smaller	**større/mindre** _<u>sturr</u>´•ruh/<u>mihn</u>´•druh_	
from this region	**fra dette området** _frah <u>deht</u>`•tuh <u>ohm</u>`•<u>raw</u>•duh_	
Is it real?	**Er den ekte?** _ar dehn <u>ehk</u>`•tuh_	
Could you show me this/that?	**Kan du vise meg den/den der?** _kahn dew <u>vee</u>`•suh may dehn/dehn dar_	
It's not quite what I want.	**Det var ikke akkurat det jeg hadde tenkt meg.** _deh vahr <u>ihk</u>`•kuh <u>ahk</u>`•kew•raht deh yay <u>hahd</u>`•duh tehngkt may_	

Major credit cards are accepted at most hotels, restaurants, large shops, car rental companies and airlines, though some places will not accept them, particularly supermarkets and gas stations. It is a good idea to have some cash on hand, just in case. Traveler's checks are a safe alternative to cash, especially if you do not have a credit card.

No, I don't like it.	**Nei, jeg liker det ikke.**	nay yay <u>lee</u>´·kuhr deh <u>ihk</u>`·kuh
That's too expensive.	**Det er for dyrt.**	deh ar fohr duirt
I'd like to think about it.	**Jeg må tenke på det.**	yay moh <u>tehng</u>`·kuh poh deh
I'll take it.	**Jeg tar det.**	yay tahr deh

Paying & Bargaining

How much?	**Hvor mye koster det?**	voor <u>mui</u>`·uh <u>kohs</u>`·tuhr deh
I'll pay…	**Jeg betaler…**	yay buh·<u>tah</u>´·luhr…
in cash	**kontant**	kun·<u>tahn</u>´t
by credit card	**med kredittkort**	meh kreh·<u>diht</u>´·kohrt
by traveler's check [cheque]	**med reisesjekk**	meh <u>ray</u>`·suh·shehk
Could I have a receipt?	**Kan jeg få kvittering?**	kahn yay faw kviht·<u>teh</u>´·rihr
That's too much.	**Det er for mye.**	deh ar fohr <u>mew</u>`·uh
I'll give you…	**Jeg gir deg…**	yay yeer day…
I only have…kroner.	**Jeg har bare…kroner.**	yay hahr <u>bah</u>`·ruh… <u>kroo</u>`·nuhr
Is that your best price?	**Er det ditt siste tilbud?**	ar deh diht <u>sihs</u>`·tuh <u>tihl</u>`·bewd
Can you give me a discount?	**Kan du gi meg avslag?**	kahn dew yee may <u>ahv</u>`·slahg

For Numbers, see page 170.

Making a Complaint

I'd like...   **Jeg vil gjerne...** *yay vihl ya`r•nuh...*

  to exchange this   **bytte dette** *buit`•tuh deht`•tuh*

  to return this   **levere dette tilbake** *leh•veh`•ruh deht`•tuh*
                                tihl•bah`•kuh

  a refund   **ha pengene tilbake** *hah pehng`•uh•nuh*
                                tihl• bah`•kuh

  to see the manager   **snakke med butikksjefen** *snahk`•kuh meh*
                                buw•tihk`•shehf•uhn

YOU MAY HEAR...

Hvordan vil du betale? *voor`•dahn vihl* | How are you paying?
dew buh•tah`•luh

Kredittkortet ditt ble avslått. | Your credit card has been
kreh•diht•kurt•eht diht bleh ahv•slawt | declined.

ID, takk. *ee•deh tahk* | ID, please.

Vi tar ikke kredittkort. *vee tahr ihke* | We don't accept credit
kreh•diht•kurt | cards.

Kun kontant, takk. *kewn kun•tahnt tahk* | Cash only, please.

Har du mindre sedler? *hahr dew* | Do you have any smaller
mihn`• druh sehd`•luhr | change?

Services

Can you recommend...?	**Kan du anbefale...?**	kahn dew <u>ahn´</u>•buh•**fah**•luh.
a barber	**en herrefrisør**	ehn <u>hehr`</u>•ruh•frih•s**urr**
a dry cleaner	**et renseri**	eht rehn•suh•<u>**ree**´</u>
a hairdresser	**en frisørsalong**	ehn frih•**sur´r**•sah•lohng
a laundromat [launderette]	**et vaskeri**	eht vahs•kuh•<u>**ree**´</u>
a nail salon	**en neglesalong**	ehn <u>nay´</u>•luh•sah•lohng
a spa	**et spa**	eht spah
a travel agency	**et reisebyrå**	eht <u>ray`</u>•suh•bui•**raw**
Can you... this?	**Kan du...denne/dette?**	kahn dew... <u>dehn`</u>•nuh/ <u>deht`</u>•tuh
alter	**sy om**	sui ohm
clean	**rense**	<u>rehn`</u>•suh
mend	**lappe**	<u>lah`</u>•puh
press	**presse**	<u>prehs`</u>•suh
When will it be ready?	**Når er den/det ferdig?**	nohr ar dehn/deh <u>fa`r</u>•dih

For Grammar, see page 165.

Hair & Beauty

I'd like...	**Jeg vil gjerne ha...**	yay vihl <u>ya`r</u>•nuh h**ah**...
an appointment for today/ tomorrow	**en time i dag/i morgen**	ehn <u>tee`</u>•muh ih d**ah**g/ih <u>m**aw**`</u>•ruhn
I'd like...	**Jeg vil gjerne ha...**	yay vihl <u>ya`r</u>•nuh h**ah**...
an eyebrow/ bikini wax	**voksing av øyenbrynene/bikinilinjen**	<u>vohk`</u>•sihng ah <u>ury`</u>•uhn•bruin•uh•nuh/bih•<u>**kee**´</u>•nih•lihn•yuhn
a facial	**en ansiktsbehandling**	ehn <u>ahn`</u>•sihkts•buh•hahnd•lihng

Many luxury hotels in Norway offer spa and other health and beauty treatments. Geilo (www.geilo.no) is a popular health and wellness retreat where you can also enjoy excellent skiing.

a manicure/ pedicure	**manikyr/fotpleie** mah•nih•<u>kui</u>´r/<u>foot</u>`•play•uh
a massage	**massasje** mahs•<u>sah</u>`•shuh
some color	**litt farge** liht <u>fahr</u>`•guh
some highlights	**noen striper** <u>noo</u>`•uhn <u>stree</u>`•puhr
my hair styled	**håret stylet** <u>haw</u>´•ruh <u>stiel</u>`•uht
a hair cut	**en klipp** ehn klihp
a trim	**en stuss** ehn stews
Don't cut it too short.	**Klipp det ikke for kort.** klip deh <u>ihk</u>`•kuh fohr kohrt
Shorter here.	**Kortere her.** <u>kohr</u>`•tuhr•uh har
Do you do…?	**Tilbyr dere…?** <u>tihl</u>´•buir <u>deh</u>`•ruh…
acupuncture	**akupunktur** ah•kew•pewngk•<u>tew</u>´r
aromatherapy	**aromaterapi** ah•<u>roo</u>´•mah•teh•rah•<u>pee</u>
oxygen treatment	**surstoffbehandling** <u>sew</u>´r•stohf•buh•hahnd•lihng
Is there a sauna?	**Fins det sauna?** fihns deh <u>sev</u>´•nah

Antiques

How old is this?	**Hvor gammel er den?**	*voor gahm·muhl ar dehn*
Do you have anything of the...era?	**Har du noe fra...tiden?**	*hahr dew noo`·uh fra... tee´·duhn*
Do I have to fill out any forms?	**Må jeg fylle ut noen skjemaer?**	*maw yay fyll·eh ev nu·ehn sheh·mah·ehr*
Will I have problems with customs?	**Tror du jeg kan få problemer i tollen?**	*troor dew yay kahn faw pru·bleh´·muhr ih tohl´·luhn*
Is there a certificate of authenticity?	**Har du et ekthetssertifikat?**	*hahr dew et ehkt´·hehts·ser·tih·fih·kat*
Can you ship/wrap it?	**Kan du sende den/pakke den inn?**	*kahn dew seh`·nuh dehn/pahk`·kuh dehn ihn*

Clothing

I'd like...	**Jeg vil gjerne...**	*yay vihl yar`·nuh...*
Can I try this on?	**Kan jeg prøve den?**	*kahn yay prur`·vuh dehn*
It doesn't fit.	**Den passer ikke.**	*dehn pahs`·suhr ihk`·kuh*
It's too...	**Den er for...**	*dehn ar fohr...*
big/ small	**stor/liten**	*lee´·tuhn/ stoor*
short/long	**kort/lang**	*kohrt/lahng*
tight/loose	**trang/stor**	*trahng/stur*
Do you have this in size...?	**Har du denne i størrelse...?**	*hahr dew dehn`·nuh sturr`·rehl·suh...*
Do you have this... in a bigger/smaller size?	**Har du denne... i større/mindre størrelse?**	*hahr dew dehn`·nuh... ih sturr´·ruh/mihn´·druh sturr·rehl·suh*

Colors

I'd like something in...	**Jeg vil gjerne ha noe i...**	*yay vihl yar`·nuh hah noo`·uh ih...*
beige	**beige**	*behsh*
black	**svart**	*svahrt*

124

blue	**blått** *bloht*	
brown	**brunt** *brewnt*	
gray	**grått** *groht*	
green	**grønt** *grurnt*	
orange	**oransje** *u•rahng´•shuh*	
pink	**rosa** *roo´•sah*	
purple	**fiolett** *fih•u•leht´*	
red	**rødt** *rurt*	
white	**hvitt** *viht*	
yellow	**gult** *gewlt*	

YOU MAY HEAR...

Den kledde deg veldig godt. *dehn klehd•eh day vehl•dihg gawt*

That looks great on you.

Hvordan passer den? *voor•dahn pahs•ehr dehn*

How does it fit?

Vi har ikke din størrelse. *vee hahr ihk•eh dihn sturr•als•eh*

We don't have your size.

Clothes & Accessories

English	Norwegian	Pronunciation
backpack	**en ryggsekk**	ehn <u>ruig</u>`•sehk
belt	**et belte**	eht <u>behl</u>`•tuh
bikini	**en bikini**	ehn bih•<u>kee</u>´•nih
blouse	**en bluse**	ehn <u>blew</u>`•suh
bra	**en behå**	ehn <u>beh</u>`•haw
briefs [underpants]	**en underbukse**	ehn <u>ewn</u>`•uhr•buk•suh
coat	**en frakk m /kåpe f**	ehn frahk/<u>kaw</u>`•puh
dress	**en kjole**	ehn <u>khoo</u>`•luh
hat	**en hatt**	ehn haht
jacket	**en jakke**	ehn <u>yahk</u>`•kuh
jeans	**en olabukse**	ehn <u>oo</u>`•lah•buk•suh
pajamas	**en pyjamas**	ehn pui•<u>shah</u>´•mahs
pants [trousers]	**en langbukse**	ehn <u>lahng</u>`•buk•suh
panties (for women's underwear)	**undertøy**	ewnd•ar•tury
panty hose [tights]	**en strømpebukse**	ehn <u>strurm</u>`•puh•buk•suh
purse [handbag]	**en håndveske**	ehn <u>hohn</u>`•vehs•kuh
raincoat	**en regnfrakk**	ehn <u>rayn</u>`•frahk
scarf	**et skjerf**	eht shehrf
shirt	**en skjorte**	ehn <u>shoor</u>`•tuh

horts	**et par shorts** *eht pahr shawrts*
kirt	**et skjørt** *eht shurrt*
ocks	**et par sokker** *eht pahr sohk`•kuhr*
tockings	**et par strømper** *eht pahr strurm`•puhr*
uit	**en dress m /drakt f** *ehn drehss/drahkt*
unglasses	**solbriller** *soo`l•brihl•luhr*
weater	**en genser** *ehn gehn´•suhr*
weat suit	**en treningsdrakt** *ehn treh`•nihngs•drahkt*
wimming trunks	**en badebukse** *ehn bah`•duh•buk•suh*
wimsuit	**en badedrakt** *ehn bah`•duh•drahkt*
-shirt	**en T-skjorte** *ehn teh´•shu•rtuh*
ie	**et slips** *eht shlips*
ndershirt	**en trøye** *ehn trury•uh*

abric

d like...	**Jeg vil gjerne ha...** *yay vihl yar`•nuh hah...*
cotton	**bomull** *bum`•mewl*
denim	**denim** *deh´•nihm*
lace	**knipling** *knihp`•lihng*
leather	**lær** *lar*
linen	**lin** *leen*
silk	**silke** *sihl`•kuh*
wool	**ull** *ewl*
s it machine washable?	**Kan den vaskes i maskin?** *kahn dehn vahs`•kuhs ih mah•shee´n*

hoes

d like...	**Jeg vil gjerne ha...** *yay vihl yar`•nuh hah...*
boots	**støvler** *sturv`•luhr*
flat shoes	**lavhælte sko** *lahv`•hehl•tuh skoo*
high heels	**sko med høye hæler** *skoo meh hury`•uh heh`luhrl*
loafers	**mokkasiner** *muk•kah•see´•nuhr*

sandals	**sandaler** sahn•_dah_`•luhr
shoes	**sko** skoo
slippers	**tøfler** turf`•luhr
sneakers	**turnsko** tewrn`•skoo
In size...	**I størrelse...** ih _sturr_`•rehl•suh...

For Numbers, see page 170.

Sizes

small (S)	**liten** _lee_`•tuhn
medium (M)	**mellomstor** _mehl_`•ohm•st**oor**
large (L)	**stor** st**oor**
extra large (XL)	**ekstra stor** _ehks_´•trah st**oor**
petite	**liten (klesstørrelse)** leet•ehn kleh•sturr•ehls•eh
plus size	**ekstra stor** ehk•strah stur

Newsagent & Tobacconist

Do you sell English-language books/newspapers?	**Har dere bøker/aviser på engelsk?** hahr deh`•ruh _bur_`•kuhr/ah•**vee**´•suhr poh _ehng_´•ehlsk
I'd like...	**Jeg vil gjerne ha...** yay vihl _yar_`•nuh hah...
candy [sweets]	**noen godter** _noo_`•uhn _goht_`•tuhr
chewing gum	**en pakke tyggegummi** ehn _pahk_`•kuh _tuig_`•guh•gew•mi
a chocolate bar	**en sjokoladeplate** ehn shu•ku•_lah_`•duh•pl**ah**•tuh
cigars	**noen sigarer** _noo_`•uhn sih•_gah_`•ruhr
a pack/carton of cigarettes	**en pakke/kartong sigaretter** ehn _pahk_`•kuh/kahr•tohng´ sih•gah•_reht_´•tuhr
a lighter	**en lighter** ehn _lie_´•tuhr
a magazine	**et blad** eht bl**ah**
matches	**fyrstikker** _fuir_`•stihk•kuhr

a newspaper	**en avis** *ehn ah•vee´s*
a road/town map of...	**et veikart/bykart over...** *eht vay`•kahrt/bui´•kahrt aw•vuhr...*
stamps	**noen frimerker** *noo`•uhn free´•mehr•kuhr*

Photography

I like...camera.	**Jeg vil gjerne ha...** *yay vihl yar`•nuh hah...*
an automatic	**et helautomatisk kamera** *eht hehl`•ev•tu•mah•tihsk kah´•meh•rah*
a digital	**et digitalkamera** *eht dih•gih•tah´l•kah•meh•rah*
a disposable	**et engangskamera** *eht ehn´•gangs•kah•meh•rah*
I like...	**Jeg vil gjerne ha...** *yay vihl yar`•nuh•hah...*
a battery	**et batteri** *eht baht•tuh•ree´*
digital prints	**papirkopi av digitale bilder** *pah•pee´r•ku•pee ah dih•gih•tah´•luh bihl´•duhr*
a memory card	**en minnebrikke** *ehn mihn´•nuh•brihk•kuh*
Can I print digital photos here?	**Lager dere papirkopier av digitale bilder?** *lah`•guhr deh`•ruh pah•pee´r•ku•pih•uhr ah dih•gih•tah´•luh bihl´•duhr*

Souvenirs

(rose-painted) bowl	**(rosemalt) bolle** (_roo_`·suh·**mah**lt) _bohl_`·luh
candlestick	**lysestake** _lui_`·suh·stah·kuh
cardigan (with Norwegian design)	**lusekofte** _lew_`·suh·kohf·tuh
doll in native costume	**dukke med bunad** _dewk_`·kuh meh _bew_`·nahd
drinking horn	**drikkehorn** _drihk_`·kuh·hoorn
hunting knife	**jaktkniv** _yahkt_´·kneev
plate	**asjett** ah·sheht´
reindeer skin	**reinsdyrskinn** _reins_´·duir·shihn
sealskin slippers	**selskinnstøfler** _sehl_`·shihns·turf·luhr
troll	**troll** trohl
Viking ship	**vikingskip** _vee_`·kihng·sheep
wooden figurine	**trefigur** _treh_`·fih·gewr
woven runner	**rye** _rui_`·uh
Something typically Norwegian, please.	**Jeg vil gjerne ha noe typisk norsk.** yei vihl yar_`·n_ hah _noo_`·uh _tui_´·pihsk norsk
Can I see this/that?	**Kan jeg få se på denne/den der?** kahn yei foh s**eh** poh _dehn_`·nuh/dehn dar

Typical souvenirs from Norway include knit items like sweaters and cardigans, gloves and mittens. Other handcrafted pieces like silver, glassware, pottery and hand-painted wooden objects, such as bowls with rose designs, Norwegian trolls, fjord horses and viking ships abound. Art lovers will find that there are also many art galleries across the country. It is a good idea to get local recommendations on where to buy. Goat and reindeer skins as well as furs are also popular.

It's the one in the window/display case.	**Det er den i vinduet/monteren.**	*deh ar dehn ih* _vihn`•dew•uh/mohn`•tuhr•uhn_
I'd like…	**Jeg vil gjerne ha…**	*yei vihl yar`•nuh hah…*
a battery	**et batteri**	*eht baht•tuh•ree´*
a bracelet	**et armbånd**	*eht ahrm`•bohn*
a brooch	**en brosje**	*ehn broh`•shuh*
earrings	**et par øreringer**	*eht pahr ur´•ruh•rihng•uhr*
a necklace	**et halskjede**	*eht hahl`s•kheh•duh*
a ring	**en ring**	*ehn rihng*
a watch	**en klokke**	*ehn klohk`•kuh*
copper	**kobber**	*kohb`•buhr*
crystal	**krystall**	*krui•stahl´*
diamond	**diamant**	*dih•ah•mahnt´*
white/yellow gold	**hvitt/gult gull**	*viht/gewlt gewl*
pearl	**perle**	*par`•luh*
pewter	**tinn**	*tihn*
platinum	**platina**	*plah´•tih•nah*
sterling silver	**sterlingsølv**	*star´•lihng•surl*
Is this real?	**Er den ekte?**	*ar dehn ehk`•tuh*
Can you engrave it?	**Kan du få den gravert?**	*kahn dew foh dehn grah•vehrt´*

Sport & Leisure

ESSENTIAL

When's the game?	**Når går kampen?** nohr gawr <u>kahm</u>´·puhn
Where's…?	**Hvor er…?** voor ar…
the beach	**stranden** <u>strahn</u>´·nuhn
the park	**parken** <u>pahr</u>´·kuhn
the swimming pool	**svømmebassenget** <u>svurm</u>`·muh·bahs·sehng·uh
Is it safe to swim/ dive here?	**Er det trygt å svømme/dykke her?** <u>ar</u> deh truikt aw <u>svurm</u>`·muh/<u>duik</u>`·kuh har
Can I rent [hire] golf clubs?	**Kan jeg leie golfkøller?** kahn yay <u>lay</u>´·uh <u>gohlf</u>´·kurl·luhr
How much per hour?	**Hvor mye koster det per time?** voor <u>mui</u>`·uh <u>kohs</u>`·tuhr deh pehr <u>tee</u>`·muh
How far is it to…?	**Hvor langt er det til…?** voor <u>lahngt</u>´ <u>ar</u> deh tihl…
Can you show me on the map?	**Kan du vise meg det på kartet?** kahn dew <u>vee</u>`·suh may deh poh <u>kahr</u>´·tuh

Watching Sport

When's…?	**Når går…?** nohr gawr…
the basketball game	**basketballkampen** <u>bah</u>´s·kuht·bahl·kahm·puhn
the cycling race	**sykkelløpet** <u>suik</u>´·kuhl·lur·puh
the golf tournament	**golfturneringen** <u>gohlf</u>´·tewr·neh·rihng·uhn
the soccer [football] game	**fotballkampen** <u>foot</u>`·bahl·kahm·puhn
the tennis match	**tenniskampen** <u>tehn</u>´·nihs·kahm·puhn

the volleyball game	**volleyballkampen** <u>vohl´</u>•lih•bahl•kahm•puhn	
Which teams are playing?	**Hvilke lag spiller?** <u>vihl´</u>•kuh *lah*g spihl•luhr	
Where's the stadium?	**Hvor er stadion?** *voor ar* <u>stah´d</u>•yohn	
Where can I place a bet?	**Hvor kan jeg spille på hester?** *voor kahn yay* <u>spihl´</u>•luh poh <u>hehs´</u>•tuhr	

Norwegians are very active people and particularly enjoy outdoor sports. Water sports, such as boating, canoeing and fishing are popular, though skiing and hiking are the primary participant sports. In fact, Norwegians boast 4,000 years of skiing, since skis were originally developed as a means of transportation through the snow. Today, there are many ski resorts across Norway and tourist offices can recommend the nearest one for downhill skiing as well as local ski facilities for cross-country skiing. Hiking can be done almost anywhere, but if you're up for an exhilarating experience, try **brevandringer** (guided glacier walks).

Playing Sport

Where's…?	**Hvor er…?** *voor ar…*
the golf course	**golfbanen** <u>*gohlf´*</u>*•bah•nuh*
the gym	**trimrommet** <u>*trihm´*</u>*•rum•muh*
the park	**parken** <u>*pahr´*</u>*•kuhn*
the tennis court	**tennisbanen** <u>*tehn´*</u>*•nihs•bah•nuhn*
How much per…?	**Hva koster det per…?** *vah <u>kohs`</u>•tuhr deh pehr…*
day	**dag** *dahg*
hour	**time** <u>*tee`*</u>*•muh*
game	**spill** *spihl*
round	**runde** <u>*rewn`*</u>*•duh*
Can I rent [hire]…?	**Kan man leie…?** *kahn mahn <u>lay`</u>•uh…*
golf clubs	**golfkøller** <u>*gohlf´*</u>*•kurl•luhr*
equipment	**utstyr** <u>*ew´t*</u>*•stuir*
a racket	**en racket** *ehn <u>rehk´</u>•kuht*

Skiing is the most popular participant sport in Norway and the winter season runs from November to April. Summer skiing is also posisble from June to September in some high altitude resorts where mornings swooshing down the slopes can be combined with afternoon sunbathing. Major ski resorts are located in Geilo, Hafjell, Hemsedal, Lillehammer, Norefjell (the closest to Oslo) and Trysil. Other snow-oriented activities include dog-sledding, ice-fishing, skating, sleigh-riding, snowboarding, snowmobiling and tobogganing.

At the Beach/Pool

Where's the beach/pool?	**Hvor er stranden/svømmebassenget?**	voor ar strahn`•nuhn/svurm`•muh•bah•sehng•uh
s there…here?	**Fins det…her?**	fihns deh…har
a kiddie [paddling] pool	**et barnebasseng**	eht bahr`•nuh•bahs•sehng
an indoor/outdoor pool	**et innendørs/utendørs svømmebasseng**	eht ihn`•nuhn•durrs/ew`•tuhn•durrs svurm`•muh•bahs•sehng
a lifeguard	**badevakt**	bah`•duh•vahkt
s it safe…here?	**Er det trygt…her?**	ar deh truikt…har
to swim	**å svømme**	oh svurm`•muh
to dive	**å dykke**	oh duik`•kuh
for children	**for barn**	fohr bahn
want to rent [hire]…	**Jeg vil gjerne leie…**	yay vihl yar`•nuh lay`•uh…
a deck chair	**en fluktstol**	ehn flewkt`•stool
diving equipment	**dykkeutstyr**	duik`•kuh•ewt•stuir
a jet-ski	**en vannscooter**	ehn vahn`•skew•tuhr

On good summer days the temperatures in Norway can be warm enough to sunbathe and swim. There are possibilities for diving, waterskiing and windsurfing along the coast and on Norway's many lakes. White-water rafting and kayaking are an adrenaline-pumping option on the rivers in Oppland, Hedmark and Sør-Trøndelag.

a motorboat	**en motorboat** *ehn moo´·toor·bawt*
a rowboat	**en robåt** *ehn roo´·bawt*
snorkling equipment	**snorkleutstyr** *snohr`k·luh·ewt·stuir*
a surfboard	**et surfebrett** *eht sewr`·fuh·breht*
a towel	**et håndkle** *eht hohng`·kleh*
an umbrella	**en parasoll** *ehn pah·rah·sohl´*
water-skis	**vannski** *vahn`·shee*
For...hours.	**For...timer.** *fohr...tee`·muhr*

For Traveling with Children, see page 147.

Winter Sports

Can I have a lift pass for a day/five days?	**Kan jeg få et heiskort for én dag/fem dager?** *kahn yay faw eht hays`·kort fohr ehn dahg/fehm dah`g·uhr*
I'd like to rent [hire]...	**Jeg vil gjerne leie...** *yay vihl yar`·nuh lay`·uh...*
boots	**støvler** *sturv`·luhr*
a helmet	**en hjelm** *ehn yehlm*
poles	**staver** *stah`·vuhr*
skis	**ski** *shee*
a snowboard	**et snøbrett** *eht snur`·breht*
snowshoes	**truger** *trew`·guhr*

These are too big/small.	**Disse er for store/små.** <u>dihs</u>`·suh ar fohr <u>stoo</u>´·ruh/ smaw
Can I take skiing lessons?	**Kan jeg ta skitimer?** kahn yay tah <u>shee</u>´·tee·muhr
I'm a beginner.	**Jeg er nybegynner.** yay ar <u>nui</u>`·buh·yuin·nuhr
Can I have a trail [piste] map?	**Kan jeg få et løypekart?** kahn yay faw eht <u>lury</u>`·puh·kahrt

Out in the Country

Can I have a map of…?	**Kan jeg få et kart over…?** kahn yay faw eht kart <u>aw</u>´·vuhr…
this region	**dette området** <u>deht</u>`·tuh <u>ohm</u>`·raw·duh
the walking routes	**turstier** <u>tewr</u>´·stee·uhr
the bike routes	**sykkelstier** <u>suik</u>´·kuhl·stee·uhr
the trails	**skiløypene** <u>shee</u>´·lury·puh·nuh
Is it an easy/a difficult trip?	**Er det en lett/vanskelig tur?** ar deh ehn leht/ <u>vahn</u>`·skuh·lih tewr
Is it far/steep?	**Er det langt/bratt?** ar deh lahngt/braht

How far is it to…?	**Hvor langt er det til…?**
	voor lahngt´ ar deh tihl…
Can you show me on the map?	**Kan du vise meg på kartet?** *kahn dew vee`·suh m*
	poh kahr´·tuh
I'm lost.	**Jeg har gått meg bort.**
	yay hahr goht may bu·rt
Where's…?	**Hvor er…?** *voor ar…*
the bridge	**broen** *broo´·uhn*
the cave	**hulen** *hew`·luhn*
the farm	**gården** *gawr´·uhn*
the ferry landing	**ferjestedet** *fer`·yuh·steh·duh*
the field	**jordet** *yoo`·ruh*
the fjord	**fjorden** *fyoo´·ruhn*
the forest	**skogen** *skoo´·guhn*
the glacier	**breen** *breh´·uhn*
the hill	**bakken** *bahk`·kuhn*
the lake	**innsjøen** *ihn`·shur·uhn*
the mountain	**fjellet** *fyehl´·luh*
the nature preserve	**nasjonalparken** *nah·shu·nah´l·par·kuhn*

the overlook	**utsikten**	_ew`t_•sihk•tuhn
the park	**parken**	_pahr´_•kuhn
the path	**stien**	_stee´_•uhn
the peak	**toppen**	_tohp´_•puhn
the picnic area	**turområdet**	_tewr´_•um•**raw**•duh
the pond	**dammen**	_dahm´_•muhn
the river	**elva**	_ehl´_•vah
the waterfall	**fossen**	_foh´_•suhn

Culturally, there is a lot to enjoy in Norway. In summer, many cultural events, including orchestral concerts and operas, are celebrated outdoors. Theater is extremely popular, though most productions are in Norwegian. Classical ballet is performed at the Oslo Opera House and traditional folk dances can be seen across the country. If you are interested in the visual arts, the Munch museum, named after the internationally-famous Edvard Munch, in Oslo is popular. The extensive National Museum of Art, Architecture and Design is also in Oslo.

Going Out

ESSENTIAL

What is there to do at night?	**Hva kan man gjøre om kvelden?** *vah kahn mahn yur`·ruh ohm kvehl´·uhn*
Do you have a program of events?	**Har du en oversikt over ting som skjer?** *hahr de ehn aw`·vuhr·sihkt aw´·vuhr tihng sohm shehr*
What's playing at the movies [cinema] tonight?	**Hvilke filmer vises på kino i kveld?** *vihl`·kuh fihl`·muhr vee`·suhs poh khee´·nu ih kvehl*
Where's...?	**Hvor er...?** *voor ar...*
the downtown area	**sentrum** *sehn´·trewm*
the bar	**baren** *bahr´·uhn*
the dance club	**diskoteket** *dihs·ku·teh´·kuh*
What's the admission charge?	**Hva koster det å komme inn?** *vah kohs`·tuhr deh oh kohm`·muh ihn*

Entertainment

Can you recommend...?	**Kan du anbefale...?** *kahn dew ahn´·buh·fah·luh*
a concert	**en konsert** *ehn kohn·sehrt´*
a movie	**en film** *ehn fihlm*
an opera	**en opera** *ehn oo´·puh·rah*
a play	**et teaterstykke** *eht teh·ah´·tuhr·stuik·kuh*
When does it start/end?	**Når begynner/slutter det?** *norh buh·yuin´·nuhr/ slew´·tuhr deh*
What's the dress code?	**Hvordan bør man være kledt?** *voor´·dahn burr mahn va`·ruh kleht*

140

like…	**Jeg liker…** *yay <u>lee</u>´·kuhr…*
classical music	**klassisk musikk** <u>*klahs*</u>´·*sihsk mew·<u>sihk</u>´*
folk music	**folkemusikk** <u>*fohl*</u>`·*kuh·mew·sihk*
jazz	**jazz** *yahs*
pop music	**pop** *pohp*
rap	**rap** *rehp*

YOU MAY HEAR…

Vennligst skru av alle mobiltelefoner.	Turn off your cell [mobile]
<u>*vehn*</u>´·*lihkst skrew ah <u>ahl</u>`·luh*	phones.
mu·<u>bee</u>´l·tehl·uh·foo·nuhr	

Nightlife

What is there to do	**Hva kan man gjøre om kvelden?** *vah kahn mahn*
at night?	<u>*yur*</u>`·*ruh um <u>kvehl</u>´·uhn*
Can you	**Kan du anbefale…?** *kahn dew <u>ahn</u>´·buh·fah·luh…*
recommend…?	

The capital offers endless options for going out in pubs, bars, cafes and nightclubs. Many clubs offer live music and attract DJs and musicians from around the world. Oslo also has a growing jazz scene. All restaurants, bars and nightclubs are smoke-free indoors, though many set up outdoor tables in summer and protection for smokers in the winter. Keep in mind that alcohol is considerably more expensive in Norway than in other countries and many clubs enforce age restrictions.

a cabaret	**en kabaret** *ehn kahb•ahr•eh*
a club with .... Music	**en nattklubb med ... Musikk** *ehn naht•klewb me mews•ihk*
a dance club	**et diskotek** *eht dihs•ku•teh´k*
a gay club	**en homseklubb** *ehn hum`•suh•klewb*
a nightclub	**en nattklubb** *naht`•klewb*
Is there live music?	**Er det levende musikk der?** *ar deh leh`•vuhn•uh mew•sihk´ dar*
How do I get there?	**Hvordan kommer jeg dit?** *voor´•dahn kohm´•mur yay deet*
What's the admission charge?	**Hva koster det å komme inn?** *vah kohs`•tuhr deh kohm`•muh ihn*
Let's go dancing.	**La oss gå ut og danse.** *lah ohs gaw ewt oh dahn`•suh*
Is this area safe at night?	**Er dette området trygt om natten?** *ar deht•eh awm•rawd•eht trygt awm naht•ehn*

Special Requirements

ESSENTIAL

I'm here on business.	**Jeg er her i forretninger.** yay ar har ih fohr•<u>reht</u>´•ning•uhr
Here's my business card.	**Her har du visittkortet mitt.** hah hahr dew vih•<u>siht</u>´•kor•tuh miht
Can I have your card?	**Kan jeg få kortet ditt?** kahn yay faw <u>kor</u>´•tuh diht
I have a meeting with…	**Jeg har et møte med…** yay hahr eht <u>mur</u>`•tuh meh…
Where's…?	**Hvor er…?** voor ar…
the business center	**forretningssenteret** fohr•<u>reht</u>´•nihngs•sehn•tuhr•u
the convention hall	**konferansesenteret** kohn•fehr•<u>ahng</u>´•suh•sehn•tuhr•uh
the meeting room	**møterommet** <u>mur</u>`•tuh•rum•muh

On Business

I'm here to attend…	**Jeg er her for å delta i…** yay ar har fohr aw <u>deh</u>`l•tah ih…
a seminar	**et seminar** eht seh•mih•<u>nah</u>´r
a conference	**en konferanse** ehn kohn•fehr•<u>ahng</u>´•suh
a meeting	**et møte** eht <u>mur</u>`•te
My name is…	**Jeg heter…** yay <u>heh</u>`•tuhr…
May I introduce my colleague…	**La meg få presentere min kollega…** lah may foh preh•sahng•teh´•ruh mihn kohl•<u>leh</u>´•gah…
Nice to meet you!	**Hyggelig å treffes!** <u>huig</u>`•guh•lih oh <u>trehf</u>´•fuhs
I have a meeting/an appointment with…	**Jeg har et møte/en avtale med…** yay hahr eht <u>mur</u>`•tuh/ehn <u>ah</u>`•v•tah•luh meh…

I'm sorry I'm late.	**Jeg beklager at jeg er sent ute.** *yay buh•klah´•guhr aht yay ar sehnt ew`•tuh*
I need an interpreter.	**Jeg trenger en tolk.** *yay trehng´•uhr ehn tohlk*
You can reach me at the…Hotel.	**Du kan nå meg på Hotell…** *Dew kahn naw may paw hu•tehl´…*
I'm here until…	**Jeg blir her til…** *yay bleer har tihl…*
I need to…	**Jeg trenger å…** *yay trehng´•uhr oh…*
make a call	**ta en telefon** *tah ehn teh•luh•foo´n*
make a photocopy	**ta en kopi** *tah ehn ku•pee´*
send an e-mail	**sende en e-post** *sehn`•nuh ehn eh´•pohst*
send a fax	**sende en faks** *sehn`•nuh ehn fahks*
send a package (overnight)	**sende en pakke (over natten)** *sehn`•nuh ehn pahk`•kuh (aw´•vuhr naht´•tuhn)*

Norwegians tend to get right to business and don't engage in much small talk or socializing. You'll find them to be serious and direct in business dealings and in their manner of speaking in general.

Though titles and surnames are used frequently in introductions, they are usually dropped later. Greetings are accompanied by a handshake.

YOU MAY HEAR...

Har du en avtale? *hahr dew ehn <u>ah</u>`·v·tah·luh* Do you have an appointment?

Med hvem? *meh vehm* With whom?

Han/Hun er på et møte. *hahn/huhn ar poh eht <u>mur</u>`·tuh* He/She is in a meeting.

Et øyeblikk. *eht <u>ury</u>`·uh·blihk* One moment.

Her har du en stol. *har <u>hahr</u> dew ehn stool* Have a seat.

Vil du ha noe å drikke? *vihl dew hah <u>noo</u>`·uh oh <u>drihk</u>`·kuh* Would you like something to drink?

Takk for at du kom. *tahk fohr aht dew kohm* Thank you for coming.

ESSENTIAL

Is there any discount for children?	**Er det reduksjon for barn?** *ar deh reh•dewk•<u>shoo</u>´n fohr bahrn*
Can you recommend a babysitter?	**Kan du anbefale en barnevakt?** *kahn dew <u>ahn</u>´•buh•<u>fah</u>•luh ehn <u>bahr</u>`•nuh•vahkt*
Could we have a child's seat/highchair?	**Kan vi få en barnestol/babystol?** *kahn vee faw ehn <u>bahr</u>`•nuh•st<u>oo</u>l/<u>beh</u>´•bih•st<u>oo</u>l*
Where can I change the baby?	**Hvor kan jeg bytte på babyen?** *voor kahn yay buit`•tuh poh <u>beh</u>´•bih•uhn*

Out & About

Can you recommend something for the kids?	**Kan du anbefale noe for barna?** *kahn dew <u>ahn</u>´•buh•<u>fah</u>•luh <u>noo</u>`•uh fohr <u>bahr</u>´•nah*
Where's…?	**Hvor er…?** *voor ar…*
the amusement park	**fornøyelsesparken** *fohr•<u>nury</u>´•uhl•suhs•pahr•kuhn*
the arcade	**spillehallen** *spihl•eh•<u>hahl</u>•ehn*
the kiddie [paddling] pool	**plaskebassenget** *<u>plahs</u>`•kuh•bahs•sehng•uh*
the park	**parken** *<u>pahr</u>´•kuhn*
the playground	**lekeplassen** *<u>leh</u>`•kuh•plahs•suhn*
the zoo	**dyrehagen** *<u>dui</u>´•ruh•hah•guhn*
Are kids allowed?	**Er det adgang for barn?** *ar deh <u>ahd</u>`•gahng fohr bahrn*

Is it safe for children?	**Er det trygt for barn?**	*ar deh truikt fohr bahrn*
Is it suitable for... year olds?	**Passer det for...åringer?**	*pahs`•suhr deh fohr... `•awr•ihng•uhr*

For Numbers, see page 170.

Baby Essentials

Do you have...?	**Har dere...?**	*hahr deh`•ruh...*
a baby bottle	**en tåteflaske**	*ehn taw`•tuh•flahs•kuh*
baby wipes	**papirkluter**	*pah•pee´r•klew•tuhr*
a car seat	**et barnesete**	*eht bahr`•nuh•seh•tuh*
a children's menu/ portion	**en barnemeny/barneporsjon**	*ehn bahr`•nuh•meh•nui/bahr`•nuh•poor•shoon*
a child's seat/ highchair	**en barnestol/babystol**	*ehn bahr`•nuh•stool/beh´•bih•stool*
a crib/cot	**en barneseng/sprinkelseng**	*ehn bahr`•nuh•sehng/sprihng´•kul•sehng*
diapers [nappies]	**bleier**	*blay`•uhr*
formula	**morsmelkerstatning**	*moors´•mehlk•ehr•staht•nih...*
a pacifier [dummy]	**en narresmokk**	*ehn nahr`•ruh•smuk*
a playpen	**en lekegrind**	*ehn leh`•kuh•grihn*
a stroller [pushchair]	**en gåstol**	*ehn gaw´•stool*

Can I breastfeed the baby here?	**Kan jeg amme babyen her?** *kahn yay ahm`·uh beh´·bih·uhn har*
Where can I change the baby?	**Hvor kan jeg bytte på babyen?** *voor kahn yay buit`·tuh poh beh´·bih·uhn*

For Dining with Children, see page 63.

Babysitting

Can you recommend a reliable babysitter?	**Kan du anbefale en pålitelig barnevakt?** *kahn dew ahn´·buh·fah·luh ehn poh·lee´·tuh·lih bahr`·nuh·vahkt*
What's the charge?	**Hvor mye koster det?** *voor mui`·uh kohs`·tuhr deh*
We'll be back by…	**Vi er tilbake klokken…** *vee ar tihl·bah´·kuh klohk`·kuhn…*
I'll be back by…	**Jeg er tilbake til…** *yay ar tihl·bahk·eh tih*
I can be reached at…	**Jeg kan nås på…** *yay kahn naws poh…*
If you need to contact me, call…	**Om du må kontakte meg, ring…** *Awm dew maw kun·takht·eh may rihng*

Health & Emergency

Can you recommend a pediatrician?	**Kan du anbefale en barnelege?** *kahn dew ahn´·buh·fah·luh ehn bahr`·nuh·leh·guh*
My child is allergic to…	**Barnet mitt er allergisk mot…** *bahr´·nuh miht ar ah·lehr´·gihsk moot…*
My child is missing.	**Barnet mitt er kommet bort.** *bahr´·nuh miht ar kohm`·muht boort*
Have you seen a boy/girl?	**Har du sett en gutt/jente?** *hahr dew seht ehn gewt/yehn`·tuh*

For Police, see page 154.

For Pharmacy, see page 161.

Disabled Travelers

ESSENTIAL

Is there...?	**Er det...?** *ar deh...*
access for the disabled	**adkomst for bevegelseshemmede** *<u>ahd</u>`·kohmst fohr buh·<u>**veh**</u>´·guhl·suhs·hem·muhd·uh*
a wheelchair ramp	**en rullestolsrampe** *ehn <u>rewl</u>`·luh·st**oo**ls·rahm·puh*
a handicapped- [disabled-] accessible toilet	**et handikaptoalett** *eht <u>hehn</u>´·dih·kehp·tu·ah·leht*
I need...	**Jeg trenger...** *yay <u>trehng</u>´·uhr...*
assistance	**hjelp** *yehlp*
an elevator [lift]	**en heis** *ehn hays*
a ground-floor room	**et rom i første etasje** *eht rum ih <u>furr</u>`·stuh eh·**tah**´·shuh*

Asking for Assistance

I'm disabled.	**Jeg er bevegelseshemmet.** *yay ar buh·<u>**veh**</u>´·guhl·suhs·hem·muht*
I'm visually/hearing impaired.	**Jeg er synshemmet/hørselshemmet.** *yay ar <u>sui</u>´ns·hehm·muht/<u>hurr</u>´·sehls·hehm·muht*
I'm unable to walk far.	**Jeg kan ikke gå langt.** *yay kahn <u>ihk</u>`·kuh gaw lahngt*
I'm unable to use the stairs.	**Jeg kan ikke bruke trappen.** *yay kahn <u>ihk</u>`·kuh <u>brew</u>`·kuh <u>trahp</u>´·puhn*

Can I bring my
wheelchair?
Are guide dogs
permitted?
Can you help me?
Can you open/hold
the door?

Kan jeg komme i rullestol? *kahn yay <u>kohm`</u>•muh*
*ih <u>rewl`</u>•luh•st**oo**l*
Er det adgang for førerhunder? *ar deh <u>ahd`</u>•gahng*
*fohr <u>**fur**`</u>•ruhr•hewn•nuhr*
Kan du hjelpe meg? *kahn dew <u>yehl`</u> •puh may*
Kan du åpne/holde døra? *kahn dew <u>awp</u>` •nuh/*
<u>hohl</u>`•luh <u>dur</u> ´•rah

In an Emergency

ESSENTIAL

Help!	**Hjelp!** *yehlp*
Go away!	**Gå vekk!** *gaw vehk*
Stop, thief!	**Stopp tyven!** *stohp <u>tui´</u>•vuhn*
Get a doctor!	**Hent en lege!** *hehnt ehn <u>leh`</u>•guh*
Fire!	**Brann!** *brahn*
I'm lost.	**Jeg har gått meg bort.** *yay h**ah**r goht may boort*
Can you help me?	**Kan du hjelpe meg?** *kahn d**ew** <u>yehl`</u>•puh may*

In an emergency, dial: **112** for the police
110 for the fire brigade
113 for medical emergencies.

Police

ESSENTIAL

Call the police!	**Ring politiet!** *ring pu·lih·tee´·uh*
Where's the police station?	**Hvor er politistasjonen?** *voor ar pu·lih·tee´·stah·shoo·nuhn*
There's been an accident/attack.	**Det har skjedd en ulykke/et overfall.** *deh har sheh ehn ew´·luik·kuh/eht aw´·vuhr·fahl*
My child is missing.	**Barnet mitt er kommet bort.** *bahr`·nuh miht ar kohm`·muht boort*
I need...	**Jeg trenger...** *yay trehng´·uhr...*
an interpreter	**en tolk** *ehn tohlk*
to contact my lawyer	**å kontakte advokaten min** *oh kun·tahk´·tuh ahd·vu·kah´·tuhn mihn*
to make a phone call	**å ta en telefon** *oh tah ehn teh·luh·foon´*
I'm innocent.	**Jeg er uskyldig.** *yay ar ew·shuil´·dih*

Crime & Lost Property

I want to report...	**Jeg vil anmelde...** *yay vihl ahn´·meh·luh...*
a mugging	**et overfall** *eht aw´·vuhr·fahl*
a rape	**en voldtekt** *ehn vohl`·tehkt*
a theft	**et tyveri** *eht tui·vuhr·ee´*
I've been robbed/ mugged.	**Jeg har blitt ranet/overfalt.** *yay hahr bliht rah`·nuht/aw`·vuhr·fahlt*
I've lost...	**Jeg har mistet...** *yay hahr mihs`·tuht...*
...has been stolen.	**...er blitt stjålet.** *...ar bliht styaw`·luht*

My backpack	**Ryggsekken min** _ruig`•sehk•kuhn mihn_
My bicycle	**Sykkelen min** _suik`•kuhl•uhn mihn_
My camera	**Fotoapparatet mitt** _foo`•tu•ahp•pah•raht•uh miht_
My (rental) car	**(Leie-)bilen min** _(lay`•uh)•beel•uhn mihn_
My computer	**PCen min** _peh`•seh•uhn mihn_
My credit cards	**Kredittkortet mitt** _kreh•diht`•kor•tuh miht_
My jewelry	**Smykkene mine** _smuik`•kuh•nuh mih`•nuh_
My money	**Pengene mine** _pehng`•uh•nuh mih`•nuh_
My passport	**Passet mitt** _pahs`•suh miht_
My purse [handbag]	**Håndvesken min** _hohn`•vehs•kuhn mihn_
My traveler's checks [cheques]	**Reisesjekkene mine** _ray`•suh•shehk•kuh•nuh mih`•nuh_
My wallet	**Lommeboken min** _lum`•muh•boo•kuhn mihn_
I need a police report for my insurance claim.	**Jeg trenger en politirapport til forsikringskravet mitt.** _yay trehng´•uhr ehn pu•lih•tee´•rahp•pohrt tihl fohr•sihk´•rihngs•krah•vuh miht_
Where is the British/American/Irish embassy?	**Hvor er den britiske/amerikanske/irske ambassaden?** _voor ar dehn breet•ihsk•eh/ahm•ehr•ee•kahn•skeh/eersk•eh ahm•bah•sahd•ehn_
I need an interpreter.	**Jeg trenger en tolk.** _yay trehng•ehr ehn tawlk_

Health

ESSENTIAL

I'm sick [ill].	**Jeg er syk.** *yay ar suik*
I need an English-speaking doctor.	**Jeg trenger en lege som snakker engelsk.** *yay trehng ´•uhr ehn <u>leh`</u>•guh sohm <u>snahk`</u>•kuhr <u>ehng´</u>•ehlsk*
It hurts here.	**Det gjør vondt her.** *deh yurr vunt har*
I have a stomachache.	**Jeg har magesmerter.** *yay hahr <u>mah`</u>•guh•smer•tuh*

Finding a Doctor

Can you recommend a doctor/dentist?	**Kan du anbefale en lege/tannlege?** *kahn dew <u>ahn´</u>•buh•**fah**•luh ehn <u>leh`</u>•guh/<u>tahn`</u>•**leh**•guh*
Can the doctor come to see me here?	**Kan legen komme hit og undersøke meg?** *kahn <u>leh`</u>•guhn <u>kohm`</u>•muh heet oh <u>ewn`</u>•nuhr•**sur**•kuh m•*
I need an English-speaking doctor.	**Jeg trenger en lege som snakker engelsk.** *yay trehng ´•uhr ehn <u>leh`</u>•guh sohm <u>snahk`</u>•kuhr <u>ehng´</u>•ehlsk*
What are the office hours?	**Når er det kontortid?** *nawr ar deh kun•<u>toor´</u>•teed*
Can I make an appointment…?	**Kan jeg få time…?** *kahn yay faw <u>tee`</u>•muh…*
for today	**i dag** *ih dahg*
for tomorrow	**i morgen** *ih <u>maw`</u>•ruhn*
as soon as possible	**så snart som mulig** *soh snahrt sohm <u>mew`</u>•lih*
It's urgent.	**Det haster.** *deh <u>hahs`</u>•tuhr*

YOU MAY HEAR...

Hva er i veien? *vah ar ih vay´·uhn*
What's wrong?

Er du allergisk mot noe? *ar dew ah·ler´·gihsk moot noo`·uh*
Are you allergic to anything?

Gap opp. *gahp ohp*
Open your mouth.

Pust dypt. *pewst duipt*
Breathe deeply.

Du bør få foretatt en allmenn undersøkelse. *dew burr foh faw´·ruh·taht ehn ahl`·mehn ewn`·nuhr·sur·kuh·uhl·suh*
I want you to go to the hospital.

Symptoms

I'm bleeding.	**Jeg blør.** *yay blurr*
I'm constipated.	**Jeg har forstoppelse.** *yay hahr fohr·stohp´·puhl·suh*
I'm dizzy.	**Jeg er svimmel.** *yay ar svihm´·muhl*
It hurts here.	**Det gjør vondt her.** *deh yurr vunt har*
I have...	**Jeg har...** *yay hahr...*
an allergic reaction	**fått en allergisk reaksjon** *foht ehn ah·ler´·gihsk reh·ahk·shoo´n*
chest pain	**vondt i brystet** *vunt ih bruis´·tuh*
cramps	**kramper** *krahm·pehr*
diarrhea	**diaré** *dee·ahr·ehn*
an earache	**øreverk** *ur`·ruh·vehrk*
a fever	**feber** *feh´·buhr*
pain	**smerter** *smer`·tuhr*
a rash	**utslett** *ew`t·shleht*
sprained...	**forstuet...** *fohr·stew´·uht...*
some swelling	**hevelse** *heh`·vuhl·suh*
a stomachache	**magesmerter** *mah`·guh·smer·tuhr*
sunstroke	**fått solstikk** *foht soo`l·stihk*

I've been sick [ill]	**Jeg har vært syk i...dager.** *yay hahr vert suik ih..*
for...days.	*dahg`•uhr*
I'm ...months	**Jeg er ...måneder gravid** *yay ar mawn•ehd•ehr*
pregnant.	*grah•veed*

Conditions

I have...	**Jeg har...** *yay hahr...*
asthma	**astma** *ahst´•mah*
arthritis	**leddgikt** *lehd`•yihkt*
high/low blood	**høyt/lavt blodtrykk** *huryt/lahvt bloo`•truik*
pressure	
a heart condition	**en hjertesykdom** *ehn yer`•tuh•suik•dohm*
I have epilepsy.	**Jeg har epilepsi.** *yay hahr eh•phi•lehp•see*
I'm allergic to	**Jeg er allergisk mot antibiotika/penicillin.** *yay*
antibiotics/penicillin.	*ah•ler´•gihsk moot ahn•tih•bih•oo´•tih•kah/*
	peh•nih•sih•leen´
I'm on...	**Jeg går på...** *yay gawr poh...*

Treatment

Do I need	**Trenger jeg resept/medisin?** *trehng•ehr yay*
a prescription/	*rehs•ehpt/meh•dee•seen*
medicine?	
Can you prescribe a	**Kan du skrive resept på en generika?** *kahn dew*
generic drug	*skrih•vuh reh•sehpt paw ehn gehn•ehri•kah*
[unbranded	
medication]?	
Where can I get it?	**Hvor får jeg tak i det?** *voor fawr yay tahk ee deh*

Hospital

| Please notify my | **Vær snill å underrette familien min.** *var snihl oh* |
| family. | *ewn`•nuhr•reht•uh fah•mee´•lyuhn mihn* |

am in pain.	**Jeg har smerter.** *yay h ahr smer` tuhr*
need a doctor/nurse.	**Jeg trenger en lege/sykepleier.** *yay trehng ´ uhr ehn leh` guh/sui kuh play uhr*
hat are the visiting ours?	**Når er det besøkstid?** *nohr ar deh buh sur ks teed*
n visiting…	**Jeg skal besøke…** *yay skahl buh sur k uh…*

entist

e broken a tooth.	**Jeg har brukket en tann** *yay h ahr bruk` kuht ehn than*
ave lost a filling.	**mistet en plombe.** *yay h ahr mihs` tuht ehn plum` buh*
ave a toothache.	**Jeg har tannpine.** *yay h ahr tahn` pee nuh*
n you fix my ntures?	**Kan du reparere gebisset?** *kahn dew reh pah reh ´ ruh guh bihs ´ suh*

ynecologist

ave menstrual amps/a vaginal fection.	**Jeg har menstruasjonssmerter/ underlivsbetennelse.** *yay h ahr mehn strew ah shoo ´ ns smer tuhr/ewn ` nuhr leevs buh tehn nuhl suh*
nissed my period.	**Jeg har ikke hatt menstruasjon.** *yay h ahr ihk` kuh haht mehn strew ah shoo ´ n*

I'm on the Pill.	**Jeg tar p-piller.** *yay ta*hr *peh`·pil·luhr*
I'm (not) pregnant.	**Jeg er (ikke) gravid.** *yay ar (ihk`·kuh) grah·vee´d*
I haven't had a period for…months.	**Jeg har ikke hatt menstruasjon på…måneder.** *yay ha*hr *ihk`·kuh haht mehn·strew·ah·shoo´n poh. maw`·nuhd·uhr*

For Numbers, see page 170.

Optician

I've lost…	**Jeg har mistet…** *yay ha*hr *mihs`·tuht…*
a contact lens	**en kontaktlinse** *ehn kun·tahkt´·lihn·suh*
my glasses	**brillene mine** *brihl`·luh·nuh mih`·nuh*
a lens	**et brilleglass** *eht brihl`·luh·glahs*

Payment & Insurance

How much?	**Hvor mye koster det?** *voor mui`·uh kohs`·tuhr de*
Can I pay by credit card?	**Kan jeg betale med kredittkort?** *kahn yay buh·tah´·luh meh kreh·diht´·kort*
I have insurance.	**Jeg har forsikring.** *yay ha*hr *fohr·sihk´·rihng*
Can I have a receipt for my health insurance?	**Kan jeg få en kvittering for sykeforsikringen?** *kahn yay faw ehn kviht·teh´·rihng fohr sui`k·uh·fohr·sihk·rihng·uhn*

Pharmacy

ESSENTIAL

Where's the nearest pharmacy [chemist's]?	**Hvor er nærmeste apotek?** *voor ar ner`•mehs•tuh ah•pu•teh´k*
What time does the pharmacy [chemist's] open/close?	**Når åpner/stenger apoteket?** *nohr aw´p•nuhr/ stehng`•uhr ah•pu•teh´k•uh*
What would you recommend for...?	**Hva anbefaler du mot...?** *vah ahn´•buh•fah•luhr dew moot...*
How much should I take?	**Hvor mye skal jeg ta?** *voor mui`•uh skahl yay tah*
Can you fill [make up] this prescription for me?	**Kan du gjøre i stand denne resepten for meg?** *kahn dew yur`•ruh ih stahn dehn`•nuh reh•sehp´•tuhn fohr may*
I'm allergic to...	**Jeg er allergisk mot...** *yay ar ah•ler´•gihsk moot...*

In Norway, the **apotek** (pharmacy) fills medical prescriptions, while the **parfymeri** (drug store) sells non-prescription items, such as toiletries and cosmetics. Most pharmacies are open during regular business hours: 9:00 a.m. to 6:00 p.m. on weekdays. Certain pharmacies may also be open on weekends and a few are open 24 hours a day.

YOU MAY SEE...

EN GANG/TRE GANGER OM DAGEN	once/three times a day
DRÅPE	drop
TABLETT	tablet
TESKJE	teaspoon
...MÅLTIDER	...meals
ETTER	after
FØR	before
mMED	with
PÅ TOM MAGE	on an empty stomach
Å SVELGE HEL	swallow whole
KAN FORÅRSAKE TRETTHET	may cause drowsiness
IKKE INNTA ORALT	do not ingest
KUN TIL UTVORTES BRUK	for external use only

What to Take

How much should I take?	**Hvor mye skal jeg ta?** voor _mui_`·uh skahl yay tah
How often?	**Hvor ofte?** voor _ohf_`·tuh
I'm taking...	**Jeg tar...** yay tahr...
Are there side effects?	**Er det noen bivirkninger?** _ar_ deh _noo_`·uhn _bee_´·vihrk·nihng·uhr
Is it safe for children?	**Er det trygt for barn?** ar deht·_eh_ trygt _fawr_ bahn

Health Problems

I'd like something for...	**Jeg vil gjerne ha noe mot...** yay vihl _yar_`·nuh ha _noo_`·uh moot...
a cold	**forkjølelse** fohr·_khur_´·luhl·suh
a cough	**hoste** _hus_`·tuh

diarrhea	**diarré** _dih·ah·<u>reh</u>´_	
insect bites	**insektstikk** <u>ihn</u>`·sehkt·stihk_	
motion [travel] sickness	**reisesyke** <u>ray</u>`·suh·**sui**·kuh_	
a sore throat	**sår hals** _sawr hahls_	
sunburn	**solforbrenning** <u>soo</u>`l·fohr·brehn·nihng_	
an upset stomach	**urolig mage** _ew·<u>roo</u>´·lih <u>mah</u>`·guh_	

Basic Supplies

I'd like...	**Jeg vil gjerne ha...** _yay vihl <u>yar</u>`·nuh h**ah**..._	
acetaminophen [paracetamol]	**paracetamol** _pah·rah·seht·tahm·**oo**´l_	
antiseptic cream	**en antiseptisk salve** _ehn ahn·tih·<u>sehp</u>´·tihsk <u>sahl</u>`·vuh_	
aspirin	**aspirin** _ahs·pih·<u>ree</u>´n_	
a bandage [plaster]	**plaster** <u>plahs</u>´·tuhr_	
a comb	**en kam** _ehn kahm_	
condoms	**kondomer** _kun·<u>doo</u>´·muhr_	
contact lens solution	**kontaktlinsevæske** _kun·<u>tahkt</u>´·lihn·suh·vehs·kuh_	
deodorant	**en deodorant** _ehn deh·u·du·<u>rahnt</u>´_	
a hairbrush	**en hårbørste** _ehn <u>haw</u>`r·burr·stuh_	

hair spray	**hårlakk** _hawr`·lahk_	
ibuprofen	**ibuprofen** _ih·bew·pru·fehn´_	
insect repellent	**et insektmiddel** _eht ihn`·sehkt·mihd·duhl_	
a nail file	**en neglefil** _ehn nayl`·uh·feel_	
a razor/disposable razor	**en barberhøvel/engangshøvel** _ehn bahr·behr´·hurv·vuhl/ehn´·gahngs·hurv·vuhl_	
razor blades	**barberblader** _bahr·behr´·blah·uhr_	
sanitary napkins	**sanitetsbind** _sah·nih·teh´ts·bihn_	
shampoo/conditioner	**en sjampo/hårbalsam** _ehn shahm´·pu/haw`r·bahl·sahm_	
soap	**en såpe** _ehn saw`·puh_	
sunscreen	**solkrem** _soo`l·krehm_	
tampons	**tamponger** _tahm·pohng´·uhr_	
tissues	**papirlommetørklær** _pah·pee´r·lum·muh·turrk·luh_	
toilet paper	**toalettpapir** _tu·ah·leht´·pah·peer_	
a toothbrush	**en tannbørste** _ehn tahn`·burr·stuh_	
toothpaste	**en tannpasta** _ehn tahn`·pahst·ah_	

For Baby Essentials, see page 148.

The Basics

Grammar

Norway has two official written, mutually comprehensible languages, **bokmål** and **nynorsk**. **Bokmål** is the most common and is used throughout this book although a traveler in Norway should expect to come across both.

Verbs

The present tense of regular verbs in Norwegian is formed by adding **-er** to the stem of the verb. The past tense is formed by **-et** or **-te**. The future is formed with **skal** or **vil** + infinitive. This applies to all persons (e.g., I, you, he, she, it, etc.). Following are the present, past and future forms of the verbs **å bytte** (to change) and **å kjøpe** (to buy).

	Present	Past	Future
bytte (to change)	**bytter**	**byttet**	**skal/vil bytte**
kjøpe (to buy)	**kjøper**	**kjøpte**	**skal/vil kjøpe**

Irregular Verbs

There are a number of irregular verbs in Norwegian; these must be memorized. Like regular verbs, however, the irregular verb form remains the same, irrespective of person(s). Following are the present, past and future conjugations for a few important, useful irregular verbs.

	Present	Past	Future
å være (to be)	er	var	skal/vil være
å ha (to have)	har	hadde	skal/vil ha
å kunne (to be able to, can)	kan	kunne	skal/vil kunne
å spørre (to ask)	spør	spurte	skal/vil spørre

Imperatives

The imperative is generally the same form as the stem of the verb:

Examples:

Bytt! Change!   **Kjøp!** Buy!   **Gå!** Go!

Nouns

Nouns in Norwegian can be common (masculine/feminine), feminine or neuter. There are no easy rules for determining the gender. It is best to learn each new word with its accompanying article.

The plural of most nouns is formed by an -**(e)r** ending (indefinite plural) or a -**(e)ne** ending (definite plural).

Examples:

common:	**biler**	cars	**bilene**	the cars
neuter:	**epler**	apples	**eplene**	the apples

Many monosyllabic nouns have irregular plurals:

en mann	a man	**menn**	men	**mennene**	the men
en sko	a shoe	**sko**	shoes	**skoene**	the shoe
et hus	a house	**hus**	houses	**husene**	the hous
et barn	a child	**barn**	children	**barna**	the child

Possession is shown by adding -**s** (singular and plural). Note that there is no apostrophe.

Examples:

Johns bror	John's brother
hotellets eier	the owner of the hotel
barnas far	the children's father

Articles

The article (a, an, the) shows the gender of a Norwegian noun, which can be common (masculine/feminine), feminine or neuter.

Note that the majority of feminine nouns also have a common form, but usually appear in their feminine form.

. Indefinite article (a/an)

Common:	**en bil**	a car
Feminine:	**en** (*or* **ei**) **jente**	a girl
Neuter:	**et eple**	an apple

. Definite article (the)

Where in English one says 'the house', Norwegians tag the definite article onto the end of the noun and say 'house-the'. In common nouns 'the' is **-(e)n**, in feminine nouns, **a** and in neuter nouns, **-(e)t**.

Examples:

Common:	**bilen**	the car
Feminine:	**jenta**	the girl
Neuter:	**eplet**	the apple

Personal Pronouns

I	**jeg**
you	**du**
he	**han**
she	**hun**
it	**den/det**
we	**vi**
you (plural)	**dere**
they	**de**

The two forms for 'it' refer to the gender. **Den** refers to masculine and femini nouns, **det** to neuter nouns.

Norwegian has two forms for 'you': **du** (informal) and **De** (formal). However, today, the use of the formal **De** has practically disappeared from the languag

Negatives

Negation is expressed by using the adverb **ikke** (not). It is usually placed immediately after the verb in a main clause. In compound tenses, **ikke** appe between the auxiliary and the main verb.

Jeg snakker norsk.	I speak Norwegian.
Jeg snakker ikke norsk.	I do not speak Norwegian.

Questions

Questions are generally formed by reversing the order of the subject and the verb:

Examples:

Bussen stanser her.	The bus stops here.
Stanser bussen her?	Does the bus stop here?
Jeg kommer i kveld.	I am coming tonight.
Kommer du i kveld?	Are you coming tonight?

Adjectives

An adjective agrees with the noun it modifies in gender and number. For the indefinite form, the neuter is generally formed by adding **-t**, the plural by adding **-e**.

Examples:

(en) stor hund	(a) big dog	**store hunder**	big dogs
(et) stort hus	(a) big house	**store hus**	big houses

For the definite form of the adjective, add the ending **-e** (common, neuter a plural). This form is used when the adjective is preceded by **den, det, de** (th definite article used with adjectives) or by a demonstrative or a possessive adjective.

Examples:

den store hunden	the big dog
de store hundene	the big dogs
det store huset	the big house
de store husene	the big houses

Comparative & Superlative

The comparative and superlative are normally formed either by adding the ending **-(e)re** and **-(e)st**, respectively, to the adjective, or by putting **mer** (more) and **mest** (most) before the adjective.

Examples:

stor/større/størst	big/bigger/biggest
lett/lettere/lettest	easy/easier/easiest
imponerende/mer imponerende/	impressive/more impressive/
mest imponerende	the most impressive

Demonstrative Adjectives

A demonstrative adjective agrees with the noun it modifies in gender and number. If it doesn't refer to a noun, the neuter form is used, e.g., **Hva er det?** What is that?

	common	neuter	plural
this/these	**denne**	**dette**	**disse**
that/those	**den**	**det**	**de**

Adverbs

Adverbs are often formed by adding **-t** to the corresponding adjective.

rask/raskt	quick/quickly
langsom/langsomt	slow/slowly

NUMBERS

ESSENTIAL

0	**null**	*newl*
1	**en**	*ehn*
2	**to**	*too*
3	**tre**	*treh*
4	**fire**	*fee`·ruh*
5	**fem**	*fehm*
6	**seks**	*sehks*
7	**sju**	*shew*
8	**åtte**	*oht`·tuh*
9	**ni**	*nee*
10	**ti**	*tee*
11	**elleve**	*ehl`·vuh*
12	**tolv**	*tohl*
13	**tretten**	*treh`t·tuhn*
14	**fjorten**	*fyu`·rtuhn*
15	**femten**	*fehm`·tuhn*
16	**seksten**	*says`·tuhn*
17	**sytten**	*surt`·tuhn*
18	**atten**	*aht`·tuhn*
19	**nitten**	*niht`·tuhn*
20	**tjue**	*khew`·uh*
21	**tjueen**	*khew·uh·eh´n*
22	**tjueto**	*khew·uh·too´*
30	**tretti**	*treht´·tih*
31	**trettien**	*treht·tih·eh´n*
40	**førti**	*furr´·tih*
50	**femti**	*fehm´·tih*

60	**seksti** _sehks_´•tih
70	**sytti** _surt_´•tih
80	**åtti** _oht_´•tih
90	**nitti** _niht_´•tih
100	**hundre** _hewn_`•druh
101	**hundreogen** hewn•druh•oh•**eh**´n
200	**to hundre** too _hewn_`•druh
500	**fem hundre** fehm _hewn_`•druh
1,000	**tusen** _tew_´•suhn
10,000	**ti tusen** tee _tew_´•suhn
1,000,000	**en million** ehn mihl•_yoo_´n

Ordinal Numbers

first	**første** _furr_`•stuh
second	**andre** _ahn_`•druh
third	**tredje** _trehd_`•yuh
fourth	**fjerde** _fya_`•ruh
fifth	**femte** _fehm_`•tuh
once	**en gang** ehn gahng
twice	**to ganger** too _gahng_`•uhr
three times	**tre ganger** treh _gahng_`•uhr

Time

ESSENTIAL

What time is it?	**Hvor mye er klokken?** voor _mui_`•uh ar _klohk_`•kuhn
It's noon [midday].	**Den er tolv.** dehn ar tohl
At midnight.	**Ved midnatt.** veh _mihd_´•naht
From nine o'clock to five o'clock.	**Fra klokken ni til klokken fem.** fra _klohk_`•kuhn nee tihl _klohk_`•kuhn fehm

Twenty after [past] four.	**Ti på halv fem.** *tee poh hahl fehm*
A quarter to nine.	**Kvart på ni.** *kvahrt poh nee*
5:30 a.m./p.m.	**Fem tretti/Sytten tretti.** *fehm treht´·tih/surt`·tuh treht´·tih*
Half past five.	**Halv seks.** *hahl sehks*

Days

ESSENTIAL

Monday	**mandag** *mahn´·dahg*
Tuesday	**tirsdag** *teers´·dahg*
Wednesday	**onsdag** *uns´·dahg*
Thursday	**torsdag** *tawrs´·dahg*
Friday	**fredag** *freh´·dahg*
Saturday	**lørdag** *lurr´·dahg*
Sunday	**søndag** *surn´·dahg*

Dates

yesterday	**i går** *ih gawr*
today	**i dag** *ih dahg*
tomorrow	**i morgen** *ih mawr`·uhn*
day	**dag** *dahg*
week	**uke** *ew`·kuh*
month	**måned** *maw`·nuhd*
year	**år** *awr*

Months

January	**januar** yah·new·**ah**´r
February	**februar** feh·brew·**ah**´r
March	**mars** mahrs
April	**april** ahp·**ree**´l
May	**mai** mie
June	**juni** yew´·nee
July	**juli** yew´·lee
August	**august** ev·gews´t
September	**september** sehp·tehm´·buhr
October	**oktober** ohk·taw´·buhr
November	**november** nu·vehm´·buhr
December	**desember** deh·sehm´·buhr

Seasons

spring	**vår** vawr
summer	**sommer** sohm`·muhr
fall [autumn]	**høst** hurst
winter	**vinter** vihn´·tuhr

Major holidays in Norway include **Syttende mai** (Constitution Day, May 17), which is celebrated across the country with parades, flags, music, dance and other festivities. **Sankthansaften** (St. John's Eve), Midsummer Night, is the longest night of the year and is also a fun event, traditionally celebrated with bonfires.

Holidays

January 1	**Første nyttårsdag**	New Year's Day
May 1	**Første mai**	May Day (Labor Day)
May 17	**Syttende mai**	Constitution Day
December 25	**Første juledag**	Christmas Day
December 26	**Annen juledag**	Boxing Day

Moveable Dates

Maundy Thursday	**Skjærtorsdag**
Good Friday	**Langfredag**
Easter Sunday	**Første påskedag**
Easter Monday	**Annen påskedag**
Ascension Day	**Kristi himmelfartsdag**
Whit Sunday	**Første pinsedag**
Whit Monday	**Annen pinsedag**
St. John's Eve	**Sankthansaften**

Numerous festivals and cultural events are scheduled throughout the year in Norway, some with movable dates. Tourist offices, travel agencies, hotels and guidebooks offer extensive information about local and national celebrations. Many festivals are music oriented featuring folk, chamber and opera, with jazz music being especially popular.

Conversion Tables

When you know	Multiply by	To find
ounces	28.3	grams
pounds	0.45	kilograms
inches	2.54	centimeters
feet	0.3	meters
miles	1.61	kilometers
square inches	6.45	sq. centimeters
square feet	0.09	sq. meters
square miles	2.59	sq. kilometers
pints (U.S./Brit)	0.47/0.56	liters
gallons (U.S./Brit)	3.8/4.5	liters
Fahrenheit	5/9, after 32	Centigrade
Centigrade	9/5, then +32	Fahrenheit

Mileage

1 km	0.62 mi
5 km	3.10 mi
10 km	6.20 mi
20 km	12.4 mi
50 km	31.0 mi
100 km	62.0 mi

Measurement

gram	**et gram** *eht grahm*	= 0.035 oz.
kilogram (kg)	**et kilogram** *eht khee´·lu·grahm*	= 2.2 lb
liter (l)	**en liter** *ehn lee´·tuhr*	= 1.06 U.S./0.88 Brit. quarts

1 centimeter (cm)	**en centimeter** *ehn <u>sehn</u>´·tih·meh·tuhr*	= 0.4 inch
1 meter (m)	**en meter** *ehn meh´·tuhr*	= 3.28 feet
1 kilometer (km)	**en kilometer** *ehn khee´·lu·meh·tuhr*	= 0.62 mile

Temperature

-40° C – -40° F	**5**° C – 41°F
-30° C – -22° F	**10**° C – 50° F
-20° C – -4° F	**15**° C – 59° F
-10° C – 14° F	**20**° C – 68° F
-5° C – 23° F	**25**° C – 77° F
-1° C – 30° F	**30**° C – 86° F
0° C – 32° F	**35**° C – 95° F

Oven Temperature

100° C – 212° F	**177**° C – 350° F
121° C – 250° F	**204**° C – 400° F
149° C – 300° F	**260**° C – 500° F

NORWEGIAN ALPHABET

Uppercase	Lowercase	Pronunciation as in
A	a	f**a**ther
B	b	**b**etter
C	c	**c**enter
D	d	**d**ebt
E	e	**e**ntry
F	f	**f**ine
G	g	**g**et
H	h	**h**at
I	i	s**ee**ther
J	j	**y**es
K	k	**k**ite
L	l	**l**ife
M	m	**m**ore
N	n	**n**ot
O	o	sch**oo**l
P	p	**p**art
Q	q	**qu**ick
R	r	**r**ound
S	s	**s**outh
T	t	**t**ime
U	u	ball**oo**n
V	v	**v**ery
W	w	**v**ine
X	x	**x**-ray
Y	y	**e**ntry
Z	z	**s**ome
Å	å	s**a**w
Æ	æ	b**a**t
Ø	ø	h**u**rt

A

a (common nouns) en; (neuter nouns) et
access (internet) v bruke (internett)
accessories tilbehør
accident ulykke
accommodation innkvartering
account konto
acetaminophen paracetamol
acupuncture akupunktur
adapter adapter
address adresse
admission adgang
after etter
afternoon ettermiddag
air conditioning klimaanlegg
airline flyselskap
airmail luftpost
airport flyplass
aisle midtgang
aisle seat sete ved midtgangen
all alt
allergic allergisk
allergic reaction allergisk reaksjon

allowed tillatt
alter v endre
alternate route annen rute
aluminum foil aluminiumsfolie
amazing praktfull
ambulance sykebil
American adj amerikansk; n amerikaner
amusement park fornøyelsespark
anemic blodfattig
antibiotic antibiotikum
antique antikvitet
antiques store antikvitetshandel
antiseptic cream antiseptisk salve
any noe
anyone noen
anything noe
apartment leilighet
appetizer forrett
appointment avtale
arcade spillehall
area område
area code retningsnummer
aromatherapy aromaterapi
around (nearby) rundt

| adj adjective | BE British English | prep preposition |
| adv adverb | n noun | v verb |

arrival ankomst
arrive v komme frem
arthritis leddgikt
ask v spørre
aspirin aspirin
asthma astma
at ved
ATM minibank
attack overfall
attractive tiltrekkende
automatic adj automatisk

B

baby baby
baby bottle tåteflaske
baby wipes papirkluter
babysitter barnevakt
back adv (**direction**) tilbake;
  n (**body part**) rygg
backpack ryggsekk
bag (carrier) bærepose
baggage [BE] bagasje
baggage claim bagasjemottak
bakery bakeri
bandage bandasje
bank (finance) bank
bar (place) bar
barber herrefrisør
basket (store) handlekurv
basketball basketball
bathroom bad

battery batteri
battleground slagsted
be v være
beach strand
beautiful vakker
bed seng
before før
beginner begynner
behind bak
beige beige
belt belte
best best
bicycle sykkel
big stor
bike route sykkelsti
bikini bikini
bill regning
birthday fødselsdag
black svart
bland smakløs
blanket ullteppe
bleed v blø
blind blind
blood blod
blood pressure blodtrykk
blouse bluse
blue blå
boat båt
boarding ombordstigning
boarding pass
  ombordstigningskort

book bok
bookstore bokhandel
boot støvel
boring kjedelig
botanical gardens botanisk hage
bother v plage
bottle flaske
bottle opener flaskeåpner
bowl (container) bolle
boy gutt
boyfriend kjæreste
bra behå
bracelet armbånd
break down v (car) få motorstopp
breakfast frokost
breathe v puste
bridge bro
briefs underbukse
bring v (something) ta med
British britisk
broken (bone) brukket;
 (out of order) gått i stykker
brooch brosje
broom feiekost
brown brun
bug (insect) insekt
bus buss
bus station busstasjon
bus stop bussholdeplass
business forretning
business card visittkort

business center
 forretningssenter
busy opptatt
but men
buy v kjøpe; **(treat)** by på

C

cable car n taubane
cafe kafé
call n (phone) samtale;
 v (phone) ringe
camera kamera
camp v campe
campsite n campingplass
can v (be able to) kunne;
 n (container) boks
can opener boksåpner
cancel v annullere
candlestick lysestake
car bil
car hire [BE] bilutleie
car park [BE] parkeringsplass
car rental bilutleie
car seat barnesete
carafe karaffel
card kort
cardigan (Norwegian) lusekofte
carry v bære
carry-on (luggage)
 håndbagasje
cart (shopping) handlevogn;

(luggage) tralle
carton kartong
cash v løse inn; n kontanter
cashier kasse
castle slott
cathedral domkirke
cave hule
cell phone mobil
certificate of authenticity
ekthetssertifikat
chair stol
chair lift stolheis
change v **(alter)** endre; **(baby)**
bytte på; **(transport)** bytte;
v **(money)** veksle;
n **(money)** vekslepenger
cheap billig
check (payment) sjekk;
(restaurant) regning
check in v **(airport)** sjekke inn
check-in desk
innsjekkingsskranke
check out v sjekke ut
cheers skål
cheese slicer ostehøvel
chemical toilet kjemisk toalett
chemist [BE] apotek
cheque [BE] sjekk
chest bryst
chest pain vondt i brystet
chewing gum tyggegummi

child barn
children's menu barnemeny
children's portion barneporsjon
church kirke
cigar sigar
cigarette sigarett
cinema [BE] kino
city by
classical music klassisk musikk
clean adj ren; v vaske
cleaning supplies
rengjøringsmidler
clear v **(ATM)** slette
cliff klippe
cling film [BE] plastfolie
close v stenge
closed stengt
clothing store klesbutikk
coat (man's) frakk;
(woman's) kåpe
coin mynt
cold adj kald;
n **(illness)** forkjølelse
colleague kollega
color farge
comb kam
come v komme
computer datamaskin
concert konsert
conditioner (hair) hårbalsam
condom kondom

onference konferanse
onfirm v bekrefte
onstipation forstoppelse
ontact lens kontaktlinse
ontact lens solution
  kontaktlinsevæske
onvention hall
  konferansesenter
ontain v inneholde
ontrol n kontroll
ooking facilities
  kokemuligheter
opper kobber
orkscrew korketrekker
orner hjørne
ost v koste
ot [BE] (child's) sprinkelseng
otton bomull
ough hoste
ountry land
ountry code landkode
ountryside land
over charge inngangspenger
ream (ointment) salve
redit card kredittkort
rib (child's) barneseng
rystal krystall
up kopp
urrency valuta
urrency exchange office
  vekslingskontor

customs toll
cut v **(with scissors)** klippe
cute søt
cycling sykling
cycling race sykkelløp

D

dairy melkeprodukter
damage v skade
dance v danse
dance club diskotek
dark mørk
day dag
deaf døv
deck chair fluktstol
declare v **(customs)** fortolle
deep dyp
delay forsinkelse
delayed forsinket
delete v **(computer)** slette
delicatessen
  delikatesseforretning
denim dongeri
dentist tannlege
denture gebiss
deodorant deodorant
department store stormagasin
departure avgang
deposit (down payment)
  depositum
detergent vaskemiddel

diabetic diabetiker
diamond diamant
diaper bleie
diarrhea diarré
dictionary ordbok
diesel diesel
difficult vanskelig
digital digital
digital camera digitalkamera
digital photo digitalt bilde
digital print papirkopi av et digitalt
  bilde
dinner middag
direction retning
dirty skitten
disabled bevegelseshemmet
discount rabatt
dish *n* (**plate**) fat; (**food**) rett
dish detergent oppvaskmiddel
dishwasher oppvaskmaskin
display case monter
disposable camera
  engangskamera
disposable razor engangshøvel
dive *v* dykke
diving equipment dykkeutstyr
divorced skilt
dizzy svimmel
do *v* gjøre
doctor lege
dog hund

doll dukke
dollar dollar
domestic innenlands
door dør
double dobbel
double bed dobbeltseng
double room dobbeltrom
down ned
downtown sentrum
drag lift skitrekk
dress kjole
dress code kleskode
drink *v* drikke; *n* drikk
drink menu drikkekart
drive *v* kjøre
driver's license førerkort
driving licence [BE] førerkort
drop (liquid) dråpe
drowsiness søvnighet
dry tørr
dry cleaner renseri
dummy [BE] (baby's)
  narresmokk
duty (customs) toll
duty-free tollfri

E

earache øreverk
earring ørering
east øst
easy lett

eat *v* spise
economy class turistklasse
electrical outlet strømuttak
elevator heis
e-mail *n* **(message)** e-post;
v sende e-post
e-mail address e-postadresse
emergency exit nødutgang
empty *adj* tom; *v* tømme
end *n* slutt; *v* slutte
English engelsk
English-speaking
engelsktalende
engrave *v* gravere
enjoy *v* nyte
enter *v* gå inn
equipment utstyr
escalator rulletrapp
e-ticket e-billett
excess luggage overvektig bagasje
evening kveld
event begivenhet
exchange *v* veksle
exchange rate vekslingskurs
excursion utflukt
excuse *v* unnskylde
exit *n* utgang
expensive dyr
express ekspress
express mail ekspresspost
extension (phone) linje

extra ekstra
extra large ekstra stor
eye øye
eyebrow øyenbryn

F

face ansikt
facial ansiktsbehandling
family familie
fan (appliance) vifte
far langt
farm bondegård
fast hurtig
fax *n* faks; *v* fakse
fax number faksnummer
fee gebyr
feed *v* mate
ferry ferge
ferry landing fergested
fever feber
field jorde
fill (a prescription) *v* gjøre i stand
fill out *v* fylle ut
fill up *v* fylle
filling (tooth) plombe
fine (OK) bra
fire (open) ild; **(disaster)** brann
fire door branndør
first class første klasse
fit *v* passe
fitting room prøverom

fix v reparere
fjord fjord
flight flyavgang
floor etasje
flower blomst
folk music folkemusikk
food mat
foot fot
football [BE] fotball
football game [BE] fotballkamp
for for
forest skog
fork gaffel
form (document) skjema
formula morsmelkerstatning
fountain fontene
free fri
freezer fryser
fresh fersk
friend venn
from fra
frying pan stekepanne
full full
full time heltid

G

game (match) kamp
garbage bag søppelsekk
garden hage
gas (car) bensin
gas station bensinstasjon

gate utgang
get v **(find)** få tak i
get off v gå av
get to v komme til
gift gave
gift shop gavebutikk
girl jente
girlfriend kjæreste
give v gi
glacier bre
glass (drinking) glass
glasses (optical) briller
go v gå
go away v gå vekk
go out v gå ut
gold gull
golf golf
golf club golfkølle
golf course golfbane
golf tournament golfturnering
good god
good afternoon god dag
good evening god aften
good morning god morgen
good night god natt
goodbye adjø
gram gram
grandchild barnebarn
gray grå
green grønn
greeting hilsen

rocery store dagligvarebutikk
round floor første etasje
uesthouse pensjonat
uide guide
uide dog førerhund
ym trimrom

air hår
air salon frisørsalong
airbrush hårbørste
aircut klipp
airdresser frisør
airspray hårlakk
alal halal
alf halv
andbag håndveske
andicapped handikappet
ard hard
at hatt
ave v ha
ead hode
eadache hodepine
ealth food store
helsekostbutikk
ealth insurance sykeforsikring
earing impaired
hørselshemmet
eart hjerte
eart condition hjertesykdom
eat varme

heater varmeovn
heavy tung
heel hæl
hello hallo
helmet hjelm
help n hjelp; v **(assist)** hjelpe;
(**oneself**) ta selv
here her
high høy
highchair babystol
highway motorvei
hill høyde
hire n utleie; v leie
hold on v **(phone)** vente litt
holiday helligdag; [BE] ferie
horse hest
hospital sykehus
hot varm
hotel hotell
hour time
house hus
how hvordan
how far hvor langt
how long hvor lenge
how late hvor sent
how many hvor mange
how much hvor mye
hungry sulten
hurry n hastverk
hurt v gjøre vondt
husband ektemann

I

I jeg
ibuprofen ibuprofen
icy kaldt
identification legitimasjon
ill [BE] syk
important viktig
impressive imponerende
in i
include v inkludere
indoor pool innendørs svømmebasseng
inexpensive rimelig
information informasjon
information desk informasjonsskranke
insect insekt
insect bite insektstikk
insect repellent insektmiddel
insert v sette inn
inside inni
instant messenger lynmelder
insurance forsikring
insurance claim forsikringskrav
interesting interessant
international internasjonal
internet internett
internet cafe internettkafé
interpreter tolk
intersection veikryss
introduce v (person)

presentere
iron (clothing) strykejern

J

jacket jakke
jazz jazz
jeans olabukse
jet-ski vannscooter
jeweler gullsmed
jewelry smykker
join v (go with somebody) bli med
just (only) bare

K

keep v beholde
key nøkkel
key card nøkkelkort
kiddie pool plaskebasseng
kilo kilo
kilometer kilometer
kiss v kysse
knife kniv
know v (something) vite; (somebody) kjenne
kosher koscher
krone (Norwegian currency) krone

L

lace knipling
lactose intolerant

laktoseintolerant
ake innsjø
anguage språk
arge stor
ast sist
ate sen
ater senere
aunderette [BE]
selvbetjeningsvaskeri
aundromat
selvbetjeningsvaskeri
aundry (place) vaskeri;
(clothes) vask
aundry facilities
vaskemuligheter
awyer advokat
ather lær
eave v **(depart)** dra;
(deposit) legge igjen
eave alone v la være i fred
eft (direction) venstre;
(remaining) igjen
ens (for glasses) glass
ess mindre
esson time
tter brev
brary bibliotek
fe boat livbåt
fe jacket flytevest
feguard badevakt
ft [BE] (elevator) heis

lift pass heiskort
light adj **(weight)** lett;
adj **(color)** lys; n lys
light bulb lyspære
lighter lighter
like v like
line linje
linen (cloth) lin
liquor store vinmonopol
liter liter
little (some) litt
live v **(exist)** leve; **(reside)** bo
live music levende musikk
loafers mokkasiner
local lokal
lock lås
log in v logge seg inn
log off v logge seg av
log on v logge seg på
long lang
look n titt; v se
lose v miste
loud (voice) høy
love v elske
low lav
luggage bagasje
luggage cart bagasjetralle
luggage locker
oppbevaringsboks
luggage trolley [BE] bagasjetralle
lunch lunsj

M

machine maskin

machine washable
  maskinvaskbar

magazine blad

magnificent storslagen

mail post

mailbox postkasse

make v lage

make up (a prescription) [BE]
  v gjøre i stand

mall kjøpesenter

man mann; (gentleman) herre

manager (shop) butikksjef

manicure manikyr

many mange

map kart

market marked

married gift

mass (church) messe

match (matchstick) fyrstikk;
  (sport) kamp

massage massasje

may (can) kunne

meal måltid

mean v bety

measuring cup målebeger

measuring spoon måleskje

medication legemiddel

medium mellomstor

meet v møtes

meeting møte

meeting room møterom

memory card minnebrikke

mend v lappe

menstrual cramps
  menstruasjonssmerter

menu meny

message beskjed

meter meter

microwave mikrobølgeovn

midday [BE] middag

midnight midnatt

mileage kjørelengde

minute minutt

miss v mangle

missing savnet

mistake feil

mobile (phone) mobil

moment øyeblikk

money penger

month måned

mop mopp

moped moped

more mer

morning morgen

mosque moské

motion sickness reisesyke

motorcycle motorsykkel

motorboat motorbåt

motorway [BE] motorvei

mountain fjell

outh munn
ove v flytte
ovie film
ovie theater kino
uch mye
ug v overfalle
ugging overfall
useum museum
usic musikk
ust (have to) måtte

ail (human) negl
ail file neglefil
ail salon neglesalong
ame navn
apkin serviett
ature preserve nasjonalpark
auseous uvel
ear nær
earby i nærheten
ecklace halskjede
eed v trenge
ew ny
ewspaper avis
ext neste
ext to ved siden av
ight natt
ightclub nattklubb
o nei; **(not anything)** ikke noe
o one ingen

non-alcoholic alkoholfri
non-carbonated kullsyrefri
non-smoking (area) for ikke-røykere
noon middag
north nord
Norway Norge
Norwegian n nordmann; adj norsk
not ikke
nothing ingenting
notify v underrette
novice nybegynner
now nå
number (shoes) nummer; **(counting)** tall
nurse sykepleier

O

off av
off-licence [BE] vinmonopol
office kontor
office hours kontortid
old gammel
on på
once én gang
one en
one-way ticket enveisbillett
only bare
open v åpne; adj åpen
opera opera

opposite midt imot
optician optiker
order v **(meal)** bestille
other andre
outdoor pool utendørs
 svømmebasseng
outlet (electric) stikkontakt
overlook utsikt
overnight natten over

P

p.m. (afternoon) om
 ettermiddagen; **(evening)** om
 kvelden
pacifier (baby's) narresmokk
pack v pakke
package pakke
paddling pool [BE]
 plaskebasseng
pain smerte
pajamas pyjamas
palace slott
pants langbukse
panty hose strømpebukse
paper papir
paper towel husholdningspapir
paracetamol [BE] paracetamol
park n park; v parkere
parking lot parkeringsplass
part time deltid
pass through v være på

 gjennomreise
passport pass
passport control passkontroll
password passord
pastry bakverk
pastry shop konditori
path sti
pay v betale
peak topp
pearl perle
pediatrician barnelege
pedicure fotpleie
pen penn
penicillin penicillin
pensioner pensjonist
per day per dag
per hour per time
per kilometer per kilometer
per night per natt
per week per uke
perfume parfyme
period (menstruation)
 menstruasjon
permit v tillate
petrol [BE] bensin
petrol station [BE]
 bensinstasjon
pewter tinn
pharmacy apotek
phone telefon
phone call telefonsamtale

phone card telefonkort
phone number telefonnummer
photo foto
photocopy fotokopi
photograph fotografi
pick up *v* **(person)** hente
picnic picnic
picnic area turområde
piece stykke
pill pille; **(contraceptive)** p-pille
pillow pute
pink rosa
piste [BE] løype
piste map [BE] løypekart
place *n* **(location)** sted; **(in hostel)** plass
plaster [BE] **(bandage)** plaster
plastic wrap plastfolie
plate tallerken; **(dessert)** asjett
platform [BE] **(station)** perrong
play *n* **(theatre)** stykke; *v* spille
playground lekeplass
playing card spillkort
playpen lekegrind
please *adv* vær så snill
plunger klosettpumpe
pocket lomme
point *v* peke
point of interest severdighet
poles (ski) staver

police politi
police report politirapport
police station politistasjon
pond dam
pop music popmusikk
portion porsjon
possible mulig
post (mail) [BE] post
postage stamp frimerke
postbox [BE] postkasse
postcard postkort
post office postkontor
pot gryte
pound (British currency) pund
pregnant gravid
premium (gas) super
prepaid calling time ringetid
prescription resept
press *v* **(iron)** presse
pressure trykk
price pris
print *v* skrive ut; *n* **(photo)** kopi
problem problem
pronounce *v* uttale
pronunciation uttale
pull *v* trekke
purple fiolett
push *v* **(open)** skyve
pushchair [BE] gåstol
put *v* sette
put through sette over

Q

question spørsmål
quick rask
quickly øyeblikkelig
quiet rolig

R

racecourse [BE] travbane
racetrack travbane
racket (sport) racket
railway station [BE]
  jernbanestasjon
rain n regn; v regne
raincoat regnfrakk
rainy regnfull
rap (music) rap
rape voldtekt
rash utslett
rate (exchange) kurs
razor barberhøvel
razor blade barberblad
reach v nå
ready klar
real (genuine) ekte
receipt kvittering
receive v motta
recommend v anbefale
red rød
refrigerator kjøleskap
region område
regular (fuel) normalbensin

reindeer skin reinsdyrskinn
relationship forhold
rent v leie
rental car leiebil
repair v reparere
repeat gjenta
report n rapport; v (a crime)
  anmelde
reservation bestilling
reserve v bestille
restaurant restaurant
restroom toalett
retired (from work) pensjonert
return v (come back) komme
  tilbake; (give back) levere tilba
return ticket [BE] tur-returbillet
right (correct) rett; (direction)
  høyre
ring (jewelry) ring
river elv
road vei
road map veikart
road sign trafikkskilt
rob rane
romantic romantisk
room rom
room service romservice
round (golf) runde
round-trip ticket tur-returbillet
route rute
rowboat robåt

rubbish [BE] søppel
rubbish bag [BE] søppelsekk
ruin ruin

S

safe *adj* **(free from danger)**
trygg; *n* safe
sandals sandaler
sanitary napkin sanitetsbind
saucer skål
sauna badstue
save (computer) lagre
scarf skjerf
schedule (transport) rutetabell
scissors saks
sea sjø
sealskin slippers
selskinnstøfler
seat plass
see *v* **(watch)** se; **(meet)**
treffe; **(examine)** undersøke
sell *v* selge
seminar seminar
send *v* sende
senior citizen pensjonist
separately hver for seg
separated separert
sentence setning
serve *v* servere
service service; **(church)**
gudstjeneste

shampoo sjampo
should burde
sheet laken
ship *n* skip; *v* sende
shirt skjorte
shoe store skobutikk
shoes sko
shop butikk
shopping area handlestrøk
shopping centre [BE]
butikksenter
shopping mall butikksenter
shopping trolley [BE]
handlevogn
short kort
shorts shorts
show *v* vise
shower dusj
shrine helligdom
sick (ill) syk
side side
side effect bivirkning
sightseeing sightseeing
sightseeing tour sightseeingtur
sign *v* undertegne
silk silke
silver sølv
single (unmarried) ugift
single room enkeltrom
single ticket [BE] enveisbillett
size (clothes) størrelse;

(shoes) nummer
ski v gå på ski
skis ski
ski lift skiheis
skirt skjørt
slice skive
slippers tøfler
slow langsom
slowly langsomt
small liten
smoke røyke
smoking (area) for røykere
sneakers turnsko
snorkeling equipment
  snorkleutstyr
snow n snø; v snø
snowboard snøbrett
snowshoes truger
soap såpe
soccer fotball
soccer game fotballkamp
sock sokk
someone noen
something noe
somewhere et eller annet sted
soon snart
sore throat sår hals
sorry v beklage
south sør
souvenir suvenir
souvenir store suvenirbutikk

spa spa
speak v snakke
speciality spesialitet
spoon skje
sports idrett
sports massage
  idrettsmassasje
sprained forstuet
square plass
stadium stadion
stairs trapp
stamp v stemple;
  n **(postage)** frimerke
start v starte
station stasjon
stay v **(remain)** bli; **(reside)** bo
steal v stjele
steep bratt
sterling silver sterlingsølv
stocking strømpe
stolen stjålet
stomach mage
stomachache magesmerte
stop n **(place)** holdeplass;
  v stoppe
store (shop) butikk
store directory butikkguide
stove komfyr
straight ahead rett frem
strange underlig
stream bekk

street gate
stroller gåstol
student student
study v studere
stunning overveldende
style v (hair) style
subway T-bane
subway station T-banestasjon
suit n (man's) dress; (woman's) drakt
suitable passende
suitcase koffert
sun sol
sunburn solforbrenning
sunglasses solbriller
sunscreen solkrem
sunstroke solstikk
super (gas) superbensin
supermarket supermarked
surfboard surfebrett
swallow v svelge
sweater genser
swelling hevelse
swim v svømme
swimming pool svømmebasseng
swimming trunks badebukse
swimsuit badedrakt
symbol tegn
synagogue synagoge

T

table bord
tablet (medical) tablett
take v ta
tampon tampong
taste v smake
tax skatt
taxi drosje
taxi rank [BE] drosjeholdeplass
taxi stand drosjeholdeplass
team lag
teaspoon teskje
tell v si
temple (religious) tempel
tennis tennis
tennis court tennisbane
tennis match tenniskamp
tent telt
terminal (airport) terminal
terrible forferdelig
text n tekst; v (message) tekste
than enn
thank v takke
theft tyveri
there (place) der; (direction) dit
these disse
thief tyv
thing ting
think v (believe) tro

this denne; dette
those de
throat hals
ticket billett
ticket office billettluke
tights [BE] strømpebukse
time (period) tid;
  (occasion) gang
timetable [BE] rutetabell
tissue papirlommetørkle
to (direction) til; **(time)** på
tobacco tobakk
tobacconist tobakkshandel
today i dag
toilet [BE] toalett
toilet paper toalettpapir
tomorrow i morgen
tonight i kveld
too for
tooth tann
toothache tannpine
toothbrush tannbørste
toothpaste tannpasta
tour tur
tourist office turistkontor
towel håndkle
town by
town map bykart
town square torg
toy leketøy
toy store leketøysbutikk

track (railway) spor
traditional tradisjonell
traffic light trafikklys
trail løype
trail map løypekart
train tog
train schedule togtabell
train station jernbanestasjon
tram trikk
translate v oversette
trash søppel
travel v reise
travel agency reisebyrå
travel guide reisehåndbok
travel sickness reisesyke
traveler's check reisesjekk
trim (hair) stuss
trip tur
troll troll
trousers [BE] langbukse
try on v prøve
T-shirt T-skjorte
turn off (device) skru av
turn on (device) skru på
TV TV
type v **(computer)** skrive
typically typisk

U
ugly stygg
umbrella paraply

underground [BE] *n* T-bane
underground station [BE]
  T-banestasjon
undershirt trøye
understand *v* forstå
unleaded blyfri
until til
upset stomach urolig mage
use *n* bruk; *v* bruke
username brukernavn

V

vacation ferie
vacuum cleaner støvsuger
vaginal infection
  underlivsbetennelse
valley dal
value verdi
VAT [BE] moms
vegetarian vegetarianer
very meget
viking ship vikingskip
visit *n* besøk; *v* **(a person)**
  besøke
visiting hours besøkstid
visually impaired synshemmet
volleyball game volleyballkamp
vomit *v* kaste opp

W

wait *v* vente

waiter servitør
waitress servitør
wake *v* vekke
wake-up call vekking
walk *v* **(go)** gå; **(stroll)** spasere
wallet lommebok
want *v* ville
warm *adj* varm; *v* varme
wash *v* vaske
washable vaskbar
washing mashine vaskemaskin
watch klokke
water vann
waterfall foss
water skis vannski
weather vær
weather forecast værutsikter
week uke
weekend helg
welcome velkommen
west vest
what hva
wheelchair rullestol
wheelchair ramp
  rullestolsrampe
when når
where hvor
which hvilken
white hvit
who hvem
whole hel

widowed (man) enkemann;
  (woman) enke
wife kone
window vindu
window seat vindusplass
windsurfer seilbrett
wine list vinkart
wireless internet trådløst internett
with med
withdraw *v* **(from account)**
  ta ut
without uten
woman kvinne
wooden figurine trefigur
wool ull
work *v* **(toil)** arbeide;
  (function) virke
wrap up *v* pakke inn
write *v* skrive
wrong i veien

Y

year år
yellow gul
yes ja
yesterday i går
you du
youth hostel vandrerhjem

Z

zoo dyrehage

A

adapter adapter
adjø goodbye
adresse address
advokat lawyer
akkurat nå right now
akupunktur acupuncture
alkoholfri non-alcoholic
allergisk allergic
allergisk reaksjon allergic reaction
alt all
aluminiumsfolie aluminum foil
amerikaner n American
amerikansk adj American
anbefale v recommend
andre other
ankomst arrival
anmelde v report (a theft)
annen rute alternate route
annullere v cancel
ansikt face
ansiktsbehandling facial
antibiotikum antibiotic
antikvitet antique
antikvitetshandel antiques store
antiseptisk salve antiseptic cream
aperitiff aperitif
apotek pharmacy [chemist BE]
arbeide v work

armbånd bracelet
aromaterapi aromatherapy
asjett plate (dessert)
aspirin aspirin
astma asthma
automatisk automatic
av off
avgang departure
avis newspaper
avtale appointment

B

baby baby
babystol highchair
bad bathroom
badebukse swimming trunks
badedrakt swimsuit
badevakt lifeguard
badstue sauna
bagasje luggage [baggage BE]
bagasjemottak baggage claim
bagasjetralle luggage cart [trolley BE]
bak behind
bakeri bakery
bakverk pastry
bandasje bandage
bank bank (finance)
bar n bar (place)

barberblad razor blade
barberhøvel razor
bare just; only
barn child
barnebarn grandchild
barnelege pediatrician
barnemeny children's menu
barneporsjon children's portion
barnesete car seat
barnevakt babysitter
basketball basketball
batteri battery
be om v ask for
begivenhet event
begynner beginner
beholde v keep
behå bra
beige beige
bekk stream
beklage v be sorry
bekrefte v confirm
belte belt
bensin gas [petrol BE] (car)
bensinstasjon gas [petrol BE] station
beskjed message
best best
bestille v order (meal); reserve
bestilling reservation
besøk n visit
besøke v visit (someone)

besøkstid visiting hours
betale v pay
bety v mean
bevegelseshemmet disabled
bibliotek library
bikini bikini
bil car
billett ticket
billettluke ticket office
billig cheap
bilutleie car rental [hire BE]
bivirkning side effect
blad magazine
bleie diaper
bli v stay (remain)
bli med v join (someone)
blind blind
blod blood
blodfattig anemic [anaemic BE]
blodtrykk blood pressure
blomst flower
bluse blouse
blyfri unleaded
blø v bleed
blå blue
bo live (reside); stay (reside)
bok book
bokhandel bookstore
boks can (container)
boksåpner can opener

olle bowl
omull cotton
ondegård farm
ord table
otanisk hage botanical gardens
ra fine (OK)
rann fire (disaster)
ranndør fire door
ratt steep
re glacier
rev letter
riller glasses
ritisk British
ro bridge
rosje brooch
ruk *n* use
ruke *v* use
rukernavn username
rukket broken (bone)
run brown
ryst chest
urde should
uss bus
ussholdeplass bus stop
usstasjon bus station
utikk store [shop BE]
utikkguide store directory
utikksenter shopping mall [centre BE]
utikksjef manager (shop)
y *n* city; town

bykart town map
bytte *v* change (transportation)
bytte på *v* change (baby)
bære *v* carry
bærepose bag (carrier)
båt boat

C

campe *v* camp
camping camping
campingplass campsite

D

dag day
dagligvarebutikk grocery store
dal valley
dam pond
danse *v* dance
dansk Danish
datamaskin computer
delikatesseforretning delicatessen
deltid part time
denne this
deodorant deodorant
depositum deposit (down payment)
der there (place)
dette this
diabetiker diabetic
diamant diamond

diarré diarrhea
die breastfeed
diesel diesel
digital digital
digitalkamera digital camera
digitalt bilde digital photo
diskotek dance club
disse these
dit there (direction)
dobbel double
dobbeltrom double room
dobbeltseng double bed
dollar dollar
domkirke cathedral
dongeri denim
dra *v* leave (depart)
drakt suit (woman's)
dress suit (man's)
drikk *n* drink
drikke *v* drink
drikkekart drink menu
drosje taxi
drosjeholdeplass taxi stand [rank BE]
dråpe drop (liquid)
du you
dukke doll
dusj shower
dykke *v* dive
dykkeutstyr diving equipment
dyp *adj* deep

dyr *adj* expensive
dyrehage zoo
dør door
døv deaf

E

e-billett e-ticket
ekspert expert
ekspress express
ekspresspost express mail
ekstra extra
ekstra stor extra large
ekte real (genuine)
ektemann husband
ekthetssertifikat certificate of authenticity
elske *v* love
elv river
en a (common nouns); one
endre *v* change
engangshøvel disposable razor
engangskamera disposable camera
engelsk English
engelsktalende English-speaking
enke widowed (woman)
enkeltrom single room
enkemann widowed (man)
enn than
enveisbillett one-way

[single BE] ticket
-post e-mail
-postadresse e-mail addess
rfaren experienced
t a (neuter nouns)
t eller annet sted somewhere
t øyeblikk hold on (phone)
tasje floor
tter after
termiddag afternoon

aks *n* fax
akse *v* fax
aksnummer fax number
amilie family
arge color
at dish
eber fever
eiekost broom
eil mistake
erge ferry
erie vacation [holiday BE]
ersk fresh
lm movie
olett purple
ell mountain
ord fjord
aske bottle
askeåpner bottle opener
uktstol deck chair

fly flight
flyplass airport
flyselskap airline
flytevest life jacket
flytte *v* move
folkemusikk folk music
fontene fountain
for for; too
for røykere smoking (area)
forferdelig terrible
forhold relationship
forkjølelse cold (illness)
fornøyelsespark amusement park
forretning business
forretningssenter business center
forrett appetizer
forsikring insurance
forsikringskrav insurance claim
forsinkelse delay
forsinket delayed
forstoppelse constipation
forstuet sprained
forstå *v* understand
fortolle *v* declare (customs)
foss waterfall
fot foot
fotball soccer [football BE]
fotballkamp soccer
  [football BE] game
foto photo
fotokopi photocopy

fotpleie pedicure
fra from
frakk coat (man's)
fri free
frimerke stamp (postage)
frisør hairdresser
frisørsalong hair salon
frokost breakfast
fryser freezer
full full
fylle v fill up
fylle ut v fill out
fyrstikk match (matchstick)
fødselsdag birthday
før before
førerhund guide dog
førerkort driver's license
  [driving licence BE]
første etasje ground floor
første klasse first class
få motorstopp v break down (car)
få tak i v get (find)

G

gaffel fork
gammel old
gang time (occasion)
gate street
gave gift
gavebutikk gift shop
gebiss denture

gebyr fee
genser sweater
gi v give
gift adj married
gir n speed (cycle)
gjenta v repeat
gjøre v do
gjøre i stand v make up (prepare)
gjøre vondt v hurt
glass glass (drinking)
glass lens (for glasses)
god good
god aften good evening
god dag good afternoon
god morgen good morning
god natt good night
godter candy
golf golf
golfbane golf course
golfkølle golf club
golfturnering golf tournament
gram gram
gravere v engrave
gravid pregnant
gryte pot
grå gray
grønn green
gudstjeneste service (church)
guide guide
gul adj yellow
gull n gold

gullsmed jeweler
gult gull yellow gold
gutt boy
gå v go; walk
gå av v get off
gå inn v enter
gå på ski v ski
gå seg bort v get lost
gå ut v go out
gå vekk go away
gåstol stroller [pushchair, buggy BE]
gått i stykker broken
  (out of order)

H

ha v have
ha det travelt v be in a hurry
ha gått seg bort v be lost
hage garden
halal halal
hallo hello
hals throat
halskjede necklace
halv half
halvtime half an hour
handikappet handicapped
handlekurv basket (shopping)
handlestrøk shopping area
handlevogn shopping cart
  [trolley BE]
hans his

hard hard
haste v to be urgent
hatt hat
heis elevator [lift BE]
heiskort lift pass
hel whole
helg weekend
helligdag holiday
helligdom shrine
helsekostbutikk health food store
heltid full time
hennes her
hente v pick up (person)
her here
herre man (gentleman)
herrefrisør barber
hest horse
hevelse swelling
hilsen greeting
hjelm helmet
hjelp n help
hjelpe v help
hjerte heart
hjertesykdom heart condition
hjørne corner
hode head
hodepine headache
holde rundt hug
holdeplass stop (place)
hoste v cough
hotell hotel

hule *n* cave
hullsleiv spatula
hund dog
hurtig fast
hus house
husholdningspapir paper towel
hva what
hvem who
hver for oss separately
hvilken which
hvit white
hvitt gull white gold
hvor where
hvor langt how far
hvor lenge how long
hvor mange how many
hvor mye how much
hvor sent how late
hvordan how
hæl heel
hørselshemmet hearing impaired
høy high (tall); loud (voice)
høyde hill
høyre right (direction)
håndbagasje carry-on (luggage)
håndkle towel
håndveske handbag
hår hair
hårbalsam conditioner (hair)
hårbørste hairbrush
hårlakk hair spray

I

i in
i dag today
i går yesterday
i kveld tonight
i morgen tomorrow
i nærheten nearby
i veien wrong
ibuprofen ibuprofen
  (pharmaceutical)
idrett sports
idrettsmassasje sports massage
igjen left (remaining)
ikke not
ikke noe no (not anything)
ild fire (open)
imponerende impressive
informasjon information
informasjonsskranke
  information desk
ingen no one
ingenting nothing
inkludere *v* include
inkludert included
inneholde *v* contain
innendørs svømmebasseng
  indoor pool
innenlands domestic
inngangsbillett admission (price
inngangspenger cover charge
inni inside

nnkvartering accommodations [accomodation BE]

nnsjekkingsskranke check-in

nnsjø lake

nsekt insect, bug

nsektmiddel insect repellent

nsektstikk insect bite

nteressant interesting

nteressert interested

nternasjonal international

nternett internet

nternettkafé internet cafe

---

a yes

akke jacket

azz jazz

eg I

ente girl

ernbanestasjon train [railway BE] station

orde field

---

afé cafe

ald cold

aldt icy

am comb

amera camera

amp game; match (sport)

araffel carafe

kart map

kartong carton

kasse cash desk

kaste opp v vomit

kelner waiter

kilo kilo

kilometer kilometer [kilometre BE]

kino movie theater [cinema BE]

kirke church

kjedelig boring

kjemisk toalett chemical toilet

kjenne v know (somebody)

kjole dress

kjæreste boyfriend; girlfriend

kjøleskap refrigerator

kjøpe buy

kjøpesenter mall

kjøre v drive

kjørelengde mileage

klar ready

klassisk musikk classical music

klesbutikk clothing store

kleskode dress code

klimaanlegg air conditioning

klipp haircut

klippe n cliff; v cut (with scissors)

klokke watch

klosettpumpe plunger

knipling lace

kniv knife

kobber copper

koffert suitcase

kokemuligheter cooking facilities

kollega colleague

komfyr stove

komme v come

komme frem v arrive

komme til v get to

komme tilbake v return (come back)

konditori pastry shop

kondom condom

kone wife

konferanse conference

konferansesenter convention hall

konsert concert

kontaktlinse contact lens

kontaktlinsevæske contact lens solution

kontanter cash

konto account

kontor office

kontortid office hours

kontroll control

kopi print (photo)

kopp cup

korketrekker corkscrew

kort n card; adj short

koscher kosher

koste v cost

kredittkort credit card

krone krone (Norwegian currency)

krystall crystal

kullsyrefri non-carbonated [still BE] (drink)

kunne can; may

kurs rate (of exchange)

kveld evening

kvinne woman

kvittering receipt

kysse v kiss

kåpe coat (woman's)

L

la oss let's

la være i fred v leave alone

lag team

lage v make

lagre v save (computer)

laken sheet

laktoseintolerant lactose intolerant

land country; countryside

landekode country code

lang long

langbukser pants [trousers BE]

langsom slow

langsomt slowly

langt far

lappe v mend
lav low
lavhælt flat (shoe)
leddgikt arthritis
lege doctor
legemiddel medication
legge igjen v leave (deposit)
legitimasjon identification
leie v hire; rent
leiebil rental car
leilighet apartment
lekegrind playpen
lekeplass playground
leketøy toy
leketøysbutikk toy store
lett easy; light (weight)
leve v live
levende musikk live music
levere tilbake v return
  (give back)
lighter lighter
like v like
lin linen (cloth)
linje line (transport); extension
  (phone)
liten small
liter liter
litt little; some
  (with singular nouns)
livbåt life boat
logge seg av log off

logge seg inn log in
logge seg på log on
lokal local
lomme pocket
lommebok wallet
lunsj lunch
lusekofte cardigan (Norwegian)
lynmelder instant messenger
lys n light; adj light (color)
lysestake candlestick
lyspære light bulb
lær leather
løse inn v cash
løype trail [piste BE]
løypekart trail map
  [piste map BE]
lås lock
låse seg ute v lock oneself out

M

mage stomach
magesmerte stomachache
mange many
mangle v miss
manikyr manicure
mann man
marked market
maskin machine
maskinvaskbar machine washable
massasje massage
mat food

mate v feed
med with
meget very
melkeprodukter dairy
mellomstor medium
men but
menstruasjon period (monthly)
menstruasjonssmerter
  menstrual cramps
meny menu
mer more
messe mass (church)
meter meter
middag dinner (meal); noon
  [midday BE]
midnatt midnight
midt imot opposite
midtgang aisle
mikrobølgeovn microwave
mindre less
minibank ATM
minnebrikke memory card
minutt minute
miste v lose
mobil cell [mobile BE] phone
mokkasiner loafers
moms sales tax [VAT BE]
monter display case
moped moped
mopp mop
morgen morning

morsmelkerstatning formula
moské mosque
motorbåt motorboat
motorsykkel motorcycle
motorvei highway
  [motorway BE]
motta v receive
mulig possible
munn mouth
museum museum
musikk music
mye much
mynt coin
mørk dark
møte meeting
møterom meeting room
møtes v meet
målebeger measuring cup
måleskje measuring spoon
måltid meal
måned month
måtte v must (have to)

N

narresmokk pacifier
  [dummy BE] (baby's)
nasjonalpark nature preserve
natt night
natten over overnight
nattklubb nightclub
navn name

ned down
negl nail (human)
neglefil nail file
neglesalong nail salon
nei no
neste next
noe any; anything; something
noen anyone; some (with plural nouns); someone
nord north
Norge Norway
normalbensin regular (fuel)
norsk Norwegian
nummer number (counting); size (shoes)
ny new
nybegynner novice
nyte *v* enjoy
nær near
nærmeste nearest
nødutgang emergency exit
nøkkel key
nøkkelkort key card
nå *adv* now; *v* reach
når when

O

olabukser jeans
om ettermiddagen p.m. (afternoon)
om kvelden p.m. (evening)

om morgenen a.m.
ombordstigning boarding
ombordstigningskort boarding pass
område area; region
opera opera
oppbevaringsboks luggage locker
opptatt busy
oppvaskmaskin dishwasher
oppvaskmiddel dish detergent [washing-up liquid BE]
optiker optician
ordbok dictionary
ostehøvel cheese slicer
overfall attack; mugging
overfalle *v* mug
oversette *v* translate
overvektig bagasje excess luggage
overveldende stunning

P

p-pille pill (contraceptive)
pakke package [parcel BE]; *v* pack
pakke inn *v* wrap up
palass palace
papir paper
papirkluter baby wipes
papirkopi av et digitalt bilde digital print

papirlommetørkle tissue
paracetamol acetaminophen [paracetamol BE]
paraply umbrella
parfyme perfume
parfymeri perfumery
park *n* park
parkere *v* park
parkeringsplass parking lot [car park BE]
pass passport
passe *v* fit
passende suitable
passkontroll passport control
passord password
peke *v* point
penger money
penicillin penicillin
penn pen
pensjonat guesthouse
pensjonert retired (from work)
pensjonist senior citizen
per dag per day
per kilometer per kilometer [kilometre BE]
per natt per night
per time per hour
per uke per week
perle pearl
perrong platform [BE] (station)
picnic picnic

pille pill
plage *v* bother
plaskebasseng kiddie [paddling BE] pool
plass place (hostel); seat; square
plaster bandage [plaster BE]
plastfolie plastic wrap [cling film BE]
plombe filling (tooth)
politi police
politirapport police report
politistasjon police station
popmusikk pop music
porsjon portion
post mail [post BE]
postkasse mailbox [postbox BE]
postkontor post office
postkort postcard
praktfull amazing
presentere *v* introduce (person)
presse *v* press (iron)
pris price
problem problem
protestantisk Protestant
prøve *v* try on
prøverom fitting room
pund pound (money)
puste *v* breathe
pute pillow
pyjamas pajamas
på on (place); to (time)

R

rabatt discount
racket racket (sport)
rane rob
rap rap (music)
rapport report
rask quick
regn n rain
regne v rain
regnfrakk raincoat
regnfull rainy
regning n check [bill BE] (restaurant)
reinsdyrskinn reindeer skin
reise v travel
reisebyrå travel agency
reisehåndbok travel guide
reisesjekk traveler's check [cheque BE]
reisesyke motion sickness
ren clean
rengjøringsmidler cleaning supplies
renseri dry cleaner
reparere v fix; repair
resept prescription
restaurant restaurant
retning direction
retningsnummer area code
rett dish (food); right (correct)
rett frem straight ahead

rimelig inexpensive
ring n ring (jewelry)
ringe v call (phone)
ringetid prepaid calling time
robåt rowboat
rolig quiet
rom room
romantisk romantic
romservice room service
rosa pink
ruin n ruin
rullestol wheelchair
rullestolsrampe wheelchair ramp
rulletrapp escalator
runde round (golf)
rundt around (nearby)
rute route
rutetabell schedule [timetable BE] (transportation)
rygg back (body part)
ryggsekk backpack
rød red
røyke v smoke
røykfri non-smoking (area)

S

safe n safe; adj trygg
saks scissors
salve cream (pharmaceutical)
samtale call (phone)
sandaler sandals

sanitetsbind sanitary napkin [towel BE]

savnet missing

se *v* look; see

seilbrett windsurfer

selge *v* sell

selvbetjeningsvaskeri laundromat [launderette BE]

seminar seminar

sen late

sende *v* send; ship

sende e-post *v* e-mail

senere later

seng bed

sentrum downtown area

separert separated

servere *v* serve

service service

serviett napkin

servitør waiter, waitress

sete ved midtgangen aisle seat

setning sentence

sette *v* put

sette inn *v* insert

sette over *v* put through

severdighet point of interest

shorts shorts

si *v* tell

side side

sigar cigar

sigarett cigarette

sightseeing sightseeing

sightseeingtur sightseeing tour

silke silk

sist last

sjampo shampoo

sjekk *n* check [cheque BE]

sjekke e-post *v* check e-mail

sjekke inn check in (airport)

sjekke ut check out

sjø sea

skade *v* damage

skatt tax

ski skis

skiheis ski lift

skilt divorced

skip ship

skitrekk drag lift

skitten dirty

skive slice

skje spoon

skjema form (document)

skjerf scarf

skjorte shirt

skjørt skirt

sko shoes

skobutikk shoe store

skog forest

skrive *v* write; type (computer)

skrive ut *v* print

skru av *v* turn off (device)

skru på *v* turn on (device)

skyve v push (open)

skål saucer; cheers (a toast)

slagsted battleground

sleiv spatula

slett v clear (ATM)

slette v delete (computer)

slott castle

slutt n end

slutte v end

smake v taste

smakløs bland

smerte pain

smykker jewelry

snakke v speak

snart soon

snorkleutstyr snorkeling
  equipment

snø n/v snow

snøbrett snowboard

sokk sock

sol sun

solbriller sunglasses

solforbrenning sunburn

solkrem sunscreen

solstikk sunstroke

sommer summer

spa spa

spasere v walk (stroll)

spesialitet speciality

spille v play

spille på hester v place a bet

spillehall arcade

spillkort playing card

spise v eat

spisekart menu (printed)

spor track (railway)

springvann tap water

sprinkelseng crib
  [child's cot BE]

språk language

spørre v ask

spørsmål question

stadion stadium

starte v start

stasjon station

staver poles (ski)

sted place

stekepanne frying pan

stemple stamp

stenge v close

stengt closed

sterlingsølv sterling silver

sti path

stikkontakt outlet (electric)
  [socket BE]

stjele v steal

stjålet stolen

stol chair

stolheis chair lift

stoppe v stop

stor big; large

stormagasin department store

storslagen magnificent
strand beach
strykejern iron (clothing)
strømpe stocking
strømpebukse panty hose [tights BE]
strømuttak electrical outlet
student student
studere v study
stuss trim (hair)
stygg ugly
stykke piece; play (theater)
style v style (hair)
større bigger
størrelse size (clothes)
støvel boot
støvsuger vacuum cleaner
sulten hungry
super premium; super (gasoline)
supermarked supermarket
surfebrett surfboard
surstoffbehandling oxygen treatment
suvenir souvenir
suvenirbutikk souvenir store
svart black
svelge v swallow
svensk Swedish
Sverige Sweden
svimmel dizzy
svømme v swim

svømmebasseng swimming pool
syk sick [ill BE]
sykebil ambulance
sykeforsikring health insurance
sykehus hospital
sykepleier nurse
sykkel bicycle
sykkelløp cycling race
sykkelsti bike route
sykling cycling
synagoge synagogue
synshemmet visually impaired
sølv silver
søppel trash [rubbish BE]
søppelsekk garbage [rubbish BE] bag
sør south
søt cute
søvnighet drowsiness
såpe soap
sår hals sore throat

T

T-bane subway [underground BE]
T-banestasjon subway [underground BE] station
T-skjorte T-shirt
ta v take
ta med v bring (something)
ta med seg v take away (carry)

ta selv *v* help (oneself)
ta ut *v* withdraw (from account)
tablett tablet (medical)
takke *v* thank
tall number (counting)
tallerken plate
tampong tampon
tann tooth
tannlege dentist
tannbørste toothbrush
tannpasta toothpaste
tannpine toothache
taubane cable car
tegn symbol
tekst *n* text (message)
tekste *v* text (someone)
telefon phone
telefonkort phone card
telefonnummer phone number
telefonsamtale phone call
telt tent
tempel temple (religion)
tenke på *v* think about
tennis tennis
tennisbane tennis court
tenniskamp tennis match
terminal terminal (airport)
teskje teaspoon
tid time
til to (direction)
til until (time)

tilbake back (direction)
tilbehør accessories
tillate *v* permit
tillatt allowed
tiltrekkende attractive
time hour; lesson
ting thing
tinn pewter
titt look
toalett restroom [toilet BE]
toalettpapir toilet paper
tobakk tobacco
tobakkshandel tobacconist's
tog train
togtabell train schedule
  [timetable BE]
tolk interpreter
toll customs; duty (tax)
tollfri duty-free
tom empty
topp peak
torg town square
tradisjonell traditional
trafikklys traffic light
trafikkskilt road sign
tralle cart (luggage)
trapp stairs
travbane racetrack
  [race course BE]
treffe *v* see (meet)
trefigur wooden figurine

trekke *v* pull
trenge *v* need
treningsdrakt sweatsuit
trikk tram BE
trimrom gym
tro *v* think (believe)
truger snowshoes
trygg safe (free from danger)
trykk pressure
trøye undershirt
trådløst internett wireless internet
tung heavy
tur tour; trip
tur-returbillett round-trip [return BE ticket]
turistklasse economy class
turistkontor tourist office
turnsko sneakers
turområde picnic area
tursti walking route
TV TV
typisk typically
tyv thief
tyveri theft
tøfler slippers
tøm *v* empty
tørr *adj* dry
tåteflaske baby bottle

U

ugift single (unmarried)
uke week
ull wool
ukentlig *adj* weekly
ullteppe blanket
ulykke accident
underbukse panties, drawers, shorts
underlig strange
underrette *v* notify
undersøke *v* see (examine)
undertegne *v* sign
ungdomsherberge youth hostel
unge kid
universitet university
unnskyld! sorry!
unnskylde *v* excuse
urolig mage upset stomach
uten without
utendørs svømmebasseng outdoor pool
utenfor outside
utflukt excursion, trip, outing
utgang exit; gate
utleie hire
utsikt overlook
utsjekking check out
utslett rash
utstyr equipment
uttale *v* pronounce;

n pronunciation

vel nauseous

V

vakker beautiful

valuta currency

vandrerhjem youth hostel

vann water

vannscooter jet ski

vannski water skis

vanskelig difficult

vare goods

varm hot; warm

varme n heat [heating BE]; v warm

varmeovn heater

vask laundry (clothes)

vaskbar washable

vaske v clean; wash

vaskemaskin washing mashine

vaskemiddel detergent

vaskemuligheter laundry facilities

ved prep at, by, on; n firewood

ved siden av next to

vegetarianer vegetarian

vei road

veikart road map

veikryss intersection

vekke v wake

vekking wake-up call

veksle v change (money); exchange

vekslepenger n change (money)

vekslingskontor currency exchange office

vekslingskurs exchange rate

velkommen welcome

venn friend

venstre left

vente v wait

vente på v wait for

verdi value

vest west

vifte fan (appliance)

vikingskip viking ship

viktig important

ville want to

vindu window

vindusplass window seat

vinkart wine list

vinmonopol liquor store [off-licence BE]

vinter winter

virke v work (function)

vise v show

visittkort business card

vite v know (something)

voldtekt rape

volleyballkamp volleyball game

vondt i brystet chest pain

vær så snill please

vær weather

være *v* be
værutsikter weather forecast

ø

ørering earring
øreverk earache
øst east
øye eye
øyeblikk moment
øyeblikkelig quickly
øyenbryn eyebrow
øyenskygge eye shadow
øyensverte mascara
øyenvitne eye witness

Å

åpen *adj* open
åpne *v* open
åpningstid *v* business hours
år year
årstid season
åtti eighty

Berlitz®

speaking your language

phrase book & dictionary
phrase book & CD

Available in: Arabic, Cantonese Chinese, Croatian, Czech, Danish, Dutch,
English*, Finnish*, French, German, Greek, Hebrew*, Hindi, Hungarian*,
Indonesian, Italian, Japanese, Korean, Latin American Spanish, Mandarin
Chinese, Mexican Spanish, Norwegian, Polish, Portuguese, Romanian*,
Russian, Spanish, Swedish, Thai, Turkish, Vietnamese
*Book only

www.berlitzpublishing.com

NEXT TIME YOU TRAVEL,
PACK A BERLITZ

BERLITZ PHRASE BOOKS
Communicate easily in over 30 languages

BERLITZ HANDBOOKS
*Over 300 pages of comprehensive advice for inspiration,
planning and on-the-ground use*

BERLITZ POCKET GUIDES
*The world's best-selling pocket guides, available for over
125 destinations worldwide*

Berlitz® www.berlitzpublishing.com